Man in the Middle Voice

MARTIN CLASSICAL LECTURES

New Series, Volume 1

The Martin Classical Lectures are delivered annually
at Oberlin College
on a foundation established by his many friends
in honor of Charles Beebe Martin,
for forty-five years a teacher of classical literature
and classical art in Oberlin.

Man in the Middle Voice

NAME AND NARRATION
IN THE *ODYSSEY*

John Peradotto

PRINCETON UNIVERSITY PRESS

PRINCETON, NEW JERSEY

Copyright © 1990 by Trustees of Oberlin College
Published by Princeton University Press, 41 William Street,
Princeton, New Jersey 08540
In the United Kingdom: Princeton University Press, Oxford

Library of Congress Cataloging-in-Publication Data

Peradotto, John
Man in the middle voice : name and narration in the Odyssey /
John Peradotto.
p. cm.—(Martin classical lectures ; new ser., v. 1)
Includes bibliographical references.
1. Homer. Odyssey. 2. Odysseus (Greek mythology) in literature.
3. Names, Personal, in literature. 4. Narration (Rhetoric)
I. Title. II. Series.
PA25.M3   new ser., vol. 1
[PA4167] 883.01—dc20   90–34569

ISBN 0-691-06830-5 (alk. paper)

This book has been composed in Linotron Baskerville

Princeton University Press books are printed on acid-free paper,
and meet the guidelines for permanence and durability of the
Committee on Production Guidelines for Book Longevity of the
Council on Library Resources

Printed in the United States of America by Princeton University Press,
Princeton, New Jersey
1   3   5   7   9   10   8   6   4   2

For Erin, Monica, Noreen, and Nicole

ζωάγρι' ὀφέλλω

"MSABU, what is there in books?"

As an illustration, I told him the story from the Odyssey of the hero and Polyphemus, and of how Odysseus had called himself Noman, had put out Polyphemus' eye, and had escaped tied up under the belly of a ram. . . .

"How did he," he asked, "say the word, *Noman*, in his own language? Say it."

"He said *Outis*," I told him. "He called himself Outis, which in his language means Noman."

"Must you write about the same thing?" he asked me.

"No," I said, "people can write of anything they like. I might write of you."

Kamante who had opened up in the course of the talk, here suddenly closed again, he looked down himself and asked me in a low voice, what part of him I would write about.

"I might write about the time when you were ill and were out with the sheep on the plain," I said, "what did you think of then?"

His eyes wandered over the room, up and down; in the end he said vaguely: "*Sejui*"—I know not.

"Were you afraid?" I asked him.

After a pause, "Yes," he said firmly, "all the boys on the plain are afraid sometimes."

"Of what were you afraid?" I said.

Kamante stood silent for a little while, his face became collected and deep, his eyes gazed inward. Then he looked at me with a little wry grimace:

"Of Outis," he said. "The boys on the plain are afraid of Outis."

—Isak Dinesen, *Out of Africa*

CONTENTS

PREFACE

ποταμοῖς τοῖς αὐτοῖς ἐμβαίνομέν τε καὶ οὐκ
ἐμβαίνομεν, εἶμέν τε καὶ οὐκ εἶμεν.
—Heraclitus, frag. 49a DK

Located at the crossroads of different traditions
(philosophical, logical, and linguistic), the concept of
subject is difficult to handle and gives rise to
numerous ambiguities.
—A. J. Greimas and J. Courtés, *Semiotics and
Language: An Analytical Dictionary*

IF PART of the argument in the following pages did not so
vigorously challenge what Roland Barthes calls "the ideology of the person," the conventional view of the stable subject, of consistency and continuity of character, and of its
actions and products, I would use conventional language
and simply say "this book has been rewritten many times."
But even the unreflective language of convention here
barely masks its own paradoxes: how can we refer to this
book as "this book" if "it" has been rewritten? What is the
stable "it" that has come through the rewriting intact? Old-
fashioned philosophical questions, but to answer them
here would be to anticipate a dense and difficult argument. At this point, let them merely stand, as bait to those
who relish such questions and as irritant to those who do
not, advance notice of the problems of naming and of narration that figure so largely in what follows.

Yet, despite the inconsistency, I must say that this book
has been rewritten many times. There is at least a useful
fiction, a phenomenal truth here that must be stated.
There has, indeed, been a continuous project, an identifiable folder in my file, however often its labels and contents

have changed, for longer than I could mention without embarrassment. The labels and contents have changed with its author's predispositions, and those predispositions with the conceptual climate around him. The excursus on the discipline of classical studies in Chapter 1 attempts to define these changes and introduces the methodological framework for this particular reading of the *Odyssey*. But long ago the project began more naively, with very little of that intense reflection on the dynamics of text production and assimilation which characterizes current literary analysis. It began modestly and microtextually as a half-page note on the εἰς ὁ κε ("until") clause in *Odyssey* 11.122 and the conditions that surround it in Tiresias's prophecy. I wanted to articulate *the* definitive reading of this text, overturning and excluding what had gone before, an aspiration fostered in me by my philological training and by the winds then prevailing in the profession. Further reflection prompted a growing suspicion that the way this microtext was read could become a model mapped onto the whole, resulting in a picture of the *Odyssey* as a collision of empirical narrative traditions, one dominated by myth and another by *Märchen*. But even thus enlarged the goal was still a more or less prescriptive and univocal reading. I shall not here trace in detail the process whereby the word "definitive" faded from my critical vocabulary, or how so positivist an undertaking yielded to a more dialectical, theoretically open enterprise, or how that barren univocity was exchanged for a less domineering view of reading, but the reasons why it happened will be clear to see, especially in Chapter 1.

This book has been rewritten many times. And if I had not stopped where this book concludes, it would have continued to be rewritten, again and again. Like its subject, the *Odyssey* in the reading here advanced, it counterfeits a conclusion, but does not really end. As Paul Zumthor has said, "Nothing in lived reality is closed," and so a book that quietly contests stable subjects and obdurate definitions must also place in doubt the finality of endings (as it does most particularly in Chapter 3). In two fairly obvious senses at least, this book does not end. It has engendered in its author a host of fresh issues organically connected to this study and readily inferable by other professional readers of the *Odyssey*, but left on the drawing board for future elucidation. In that sense, it records the prolonged refinement of a cutting instrument that has still left the surface little more than merely scratched. It will, however, or so it is my hope, provoke its readers to take its bare suggestions as a prompt either to counterpoise or to continue the reading they find here.

This study may strike literary analysts outside the field of classical studies as less sophisticated than it could be, given the state of theoretical discussion. That is in part because it is designed largely for my colleagues in a profession long suspicious of theory and impatient, often justifiably so, with the self-indulgence and needless obscurity that too frequently blemishes its exercise. This book is, in part, a special plea for an enlarged definition of classical philology to include tools for textual exegesis not yet fully countenanced in the traditional repertoire, and so the rhetorical tone of this plea, guided by a genuine desire to communicate and to persuade, had to be chosen with utmost diplomacy. On the other hand, I have tried constantly to keep in mind the needs of nonspecialists, whose theoretical disappointments with what they find here may be counterbalanced, I hope, by a reading that brings them a philologist's heed of subtle and crucial discriminations of lexical and grammatical texture that will easily elude even the most scrupulous attention to gross narrative in a translated text.

Writing of this kind, like life itself, takes place mainly in the middle voice. I feel less like author than congeries or conduit, so great is the host of family, friends, colleagues, students, and institutions with a part in the production of this book. If this book were perfectly consistent both with this realization and with its own misgivings about "the ideology of the person" and the proprietary claims attending it, its author would have had to remain anonymous. But scholarly reading at its best is, I believe, a dialectical, ever incomplete social act; the name in this case functions merely as the locus of responsibility for a particular and partial view of the text, and its incompleteness implies an invitation to response.

This book has been rewritten many times. It would have been delayed yet further but for the material assistance of the Andrew V. V. Raymond Chair in Classics at the State University of New York at Buffalo. The main responsibility for liberating it from the curse of endless rewriting, however, lies with the Charles Beebe Martin Classical Lectures Committee at Oberlin College, chiefly with Nathan Greenberg, whose confidence in inviting me to lecture there forced design on flux. For this encouragement and for his and his colleagues' matchless hospitality I am most grateful. The last three of those five lectures were later delivered at Princeton University. The last three chapters here owe that audience an inestimable debt for thought-provoking comments and suggestions, most particularly from Andrew Ford, Robert Fagles, Charles Segal, and, more than all the rest, Froma Zeitlin, in the host of whose intellectual legatees I count myself a charter member. Another unselfish benefactor of so many in our profession, Bernard Knox, supported me too, saw the fitful and ingenuous origins of this project during my days at the Center for Hellenic Studies, helped me shape it with his ever sound advice, and gave me and my generation a model of humane scholarship to serve as potent antidote in moments of despair for the profession. Many other colleagues have helped too, directly and indirectly, of whom I name only a few who, by the inspiration of their own work or by their comments on mine, head the list of benefactors: Marilyn Arthur, Ann Bergren, Jenny Clay, Nancy Felson-Rubin, Ruth Finnegan, Gregory Nagy, Georgia Nugent, Piero Pucci, Peter Rose, Joseph Russo, Seth Schein, Laura Slatkin, and Jean-Pierre Vernant. When it comes to Joanna Hitchcock of the Princeton University Press, the vocabulary of praise breaks down. I cannot conceive how anyone could more fitly mix a humane and personalized concern with the intelligence and precision one looks for in a good editor. I must also thank my scrupulous copyeditor Sherry Wert for catching a number of lapses in the manuscript. And it would be impossible fully to recompense D. Elgie, whose quietly sustaining presence abbreviated this project's most arid interlude.

As the notes indicate, parts of Chapters 1 and 2 appeared in less developed versions in *Arethusa* 16, nos. 1–2 (1983), as "Texts and Unrefracted Facts: Philology, Hermeneutics and Semiotics," and in *Arethusa* 10, no. 1 (1977), as "Oedipus and Erichthonius: Some Observations on Paradigmatic and Syntagmatic Order," respectively. Revised portions of my essay "Prophecy Degree Zero: Tiresias and the End of the *Odyssey*," from *Oralità: Cultura, Letteratura, Discorso*, edited by Bruno Gentili and Giuseppe Paioni (Rome: Edizioni dell' Ateneo, 1986) appear in Chapters 2 and 3. I am grateful for permission to republish this material.

The text of the *Odyssey* used here is P. von der Muehll's (Basil 1962). The translations are my own except where otherwise indicated.

Man in the Middle Voice

Chapter 1

POLYSEMANTOR: TEXTS, PHILOLOGY, IDEOLOGY

There are no facts; only interpretations.
—Friedrich Nietzsche

Interpretation can never be brought to an end,
simply because there is nothing to interpret. There
is nothing absolutely primary to be interpreted,
since fundamentally everything is already
interpretation; every sign is, in itself, not the thing
susceptible to interpretation but the interpretation
of other signs.
—Michel Foucault, "Nietzsche, Freud, Marx"

Language is not an abstract system of normative
forms but a concrete heterological opinion on the
world. Every word gives off the scent of a
profession, a genre, a current, a party, a particular
work, a particular man, a generation, an era, a day,
and an hour. Every word smells of the context in
which it has lived its intense social life; all words and
all forms are inhabited by intentions. In the word,
contextual harmonies (of the genre, of the current,
of the individual) are unavoidable.
—Mikhail Bakhtin, "Discourse in the Novel"

To TAKE the *Odyssey* as one's topic in so distinguished a series as the Martin Classical Lectures, to try to write yet another book on a text that has known so many readers and
generated so much commentary, may indeed seem like the
height of temerity. And yet, if I exhibit a perilous rashness

here, I have plenty of company. There has been a steady stream of books on the *Odyssey* in recent years, ranging from those whose perspective combines the best in traditional philological analysis with an equally traditional humanist aesthetic, to one of the most recent additions, a Derridian, deconstructionist, intertextual reading of the poem. And there are others, and not a few, yet in the works. One may find differing explanations for this concentration on the *Odyssey*. Those attuned to current theoretical and methodological discussion would argue that this is a truly perplexed and disruptive text, and was no less so to nineteenth- and early twentieth-century philologists who, to blunt its scandal, scanned and dissected it, stratified it into earlier and later parts, better and worse parts, sifted it for inconsistencies, all in the search for an uncontaminated original to match their own implicit model of the work of art as an organic and harmonious whole, and of the human subject as a consistent and harmonious whole. In the wake of theoretical movements culminating in deconstructionism, however, this same perplexed and disruptive text becomes a paradigm for a less authoritative, less confident, more dialectical view of text production (writing), and of text reception (reading), and indeed for a more discordant view of the human subject.

If the approach in the present study shows unabashed signs of contemporary theoretical and semiotic perspectives, it is not out of any disdain for philology. On the contrary, I firmly believe that, however much philology and semiotics may now seem to be ranged against one another as polemical alternatives, the situation has to do more with the historical development of philology since the nineteenth century than with anything inherent in the nature of either philology or semiotics. A brief consideration of that history may help us understand the methodological crisis in which the profession stands,[1] a crisis that dramat-

---

[1] This discussion of the relationship between philology and semiotics is adapted from Peradotto 1983.

ically affects both the way we read and the way we expli-
cate a text like the *Odyssey.*

Philology is not, like semiotics, a philosophical position
or a method grounded in a philosophical position, at least
not one that is explicit; rather it is a set of skills and practices for the elucidation of texts. That set of skills and practices does not per se exclude semiotics. But although the
title of their national professional association still gives
American classicists the assurance that "philology" is their
middle name, within its ranks there is diminishing agree-
ment on the precise range of practices legitimately em-
braced by the term, while, outside its ranks in the world at
large, the term signifies, among the precious few who have
ever heard it, a dead or dying thing. That was not always
the case. Its parameters, less than a century ago, were
proud indeed. In the *Encyclopedia Britannica* prior to its
1926 edition, the huge entry on philology began like this:
"*Philology*: the generally accepted comprehensive name for
the study of the word (Greek, *logos*) or languages; it des-
ignates that branch of knowledge which deals with human
speech, and with all that speech discloses as to the nature
and history of man." By contrast, the article in the 1926
edition, carried up until the most recent revision of the
Britannica, reads like an obituary: "*Philology*: a term now
rarely used but once applied to the study of language and
literature. It survives in the titles of a few learned journals
that date to the 19th century. See *Linguistics*."

The profound change expressed in the transition between those two texts forces us to ask some fairly uncomfortable questions. First: Why has American classical philology so relentlessly and, I must say, successfully resisted
the inroads of current methodological inquiry arising
from ongoing philosophical reflection and interdisciplinary dialogue, an inquiry that has had such profound and
in some cases divisive effects on all other literary fields, including scriptural studies, and even on historical studies?
And why, amidst this general disregard, is semiotics a special object of revulsion? Or is "revulsion" too strong a word

for what might better be construed as a conspiracy of silence? If this hold-out position in Classics were deliberate, and I am not sure that it is—if, in other words, it were the product of informed reflection and open dialogue—it might become even more stubbornly entrenched by experiencing something like exoneration in a not imperceptible shift in literary studies outside classics—paralleling those in politics, religion, economics, and cultural criticism in the 1980s—away from structural and poststructural perspectives and formats toward traditional claims for philosophical realism, humanism, "determinacy of meaning," normativeness of authorial intention, and the primacy of objectivity found in the works of such critics as E. D. Hirsch, M. H. Abrams, and Gerald Graff.

A second and related question, posed to assist in answering the first: Why did classical philology, which was so intimately associated with hermeneutics in the early nineteenth century that at one stage they were virtually indistinguishable, find itself by the latter half of the century and right up to the present so far removed from the development, concerns, and goals of hermeneutics? One would have thought that philology's resistance to method on the surface should have attracted it to the fairly consistent antimethodist tendency in hermeneutics. One thinks immediately of Housman's and Wilamowitz's diatribes against it.[2]

A third question: Why did a similar marriage and sub-

---

[2] Housman 1972: 3:1059 (= *Proceedings of the Classical Association* 18 [1922]: 68): "A textual critic engaged upon his business is . . . like a dog hunting for fleas." Compare, at greater length, Wilamowitz (cited by William Calder III in "Ulrich von Wilamowitz-Moellendorff to Wolfgang Schadewaldt on the Classic," *Greek, Roman and Byzantine Studies* 16 [1975]: 452): "Why, this prized 'philological method'? There simply isn't any— any more than a method to catch fish. The whale is harpooned; the herring caught in a net; minnows are trapped; the salmon speared; trout caught on a fly. Where do you find *the* method to catch fish? And hunting? I suppose there is something like a method there? Why, ladies and gentlemen, there is a difference between hunting lions and catching fleas!"

sequent divorce occur, this time involving anthropology around the turn of the twentieth century, with the work of Frazer and the so-called.Cambridge School of anthropology? It appears that as soon as anthropology begins to develop what it considers more rigorous standards and methodologies than those employed in the nineteenth century, or at least becomes increasingly reflective about its epistemological perspectives and cultural assumptions, the classical community parts company, later to rejoin the dialogue, but then only in France on anything like a regular and fully countenanced basis.

A fourth question: Why has the discipline of classical studies, with what looks like reverse alchemy, seeking lead for gold, consistently favored the conversion of philosophy into the *history* of philosophy, rhetoric into the *history* of rhetoric, texts into the *history* of texts, mythic narratives into *historical* "evidence"? And in translation (which is, after all, practical hermeneutics), why has it preferred, at least since the mid-nineteenth century, the literal and the prosaic? Charting the course of any random passage of Homer from Chapman (1591) through Dryden (1693), Pope (1715), and Cowper (1791), to Lang, Leaf, and Myers (1883) is like ending a sumptuous feast with a dessert of thin gruel.

It should perhaps be made clear that my first question, on the resistance of classical studies to current methodological discussion, has mainly to do with the American scene. The resistance there is acknowledged to be more entrenched. Part of the reason for this may well be that American classicists, unlike their European counterparts, are physically removed from the stage where the latest scenes in the continuing history of philosophical hermeneutics and epistemology are enacted. Even their American colleagues in other European literary disciplines have at least the advantage that their subject area includes a more or less continuous literary history right up to the present, a history that parallels and frequently intersects the history of European philosophy. Now I do not wish to be misunderstood as asserting that there are no American classicists interested in or influenced by contemporary theoretical developments. Far from it. There is some first-rate work being done. What I am talking about is rather the general character of the discipline, the way in which it is defined by the content and form of the curriculum in its graduate training,[3] by the character of its professional associations, by its longest established and most prestigious journals. On this last point, were one to page through the *Transactions and Proceedings of the American Philological Association*, the *American Journal of Philology*, and *Classical Philology* over, say, the last fifteen years, it might be assumed, for all their contents show, that there was little interest in philosophy after Plotinus; that there was little interest in anthropology after, say, 1920; that there was no need to reflect openly on the presuppositions and assumptions of one's method (or lack of method); that the whole complex of twentieth-century developments in philosophy of language, phenomenology, epistemology, and historical understanding had been disregarded as irrelevant to the practical determination of verbal meaning and the reconstruction of the past. The hermeneutist of the thirty-fifth century, faced with these texts, might well wonder how the intellectual successors of Richard Bentley, at whose home John Evelyn, Christopher Wren, John Locke, and Isaac Newton met twice weekly, could give such consistent evidence of speaking to no one but members of their own profession.

Before going on, I should like to make a tangential but crucial point about this whole subject. How the profession is defined in terms of its cognitive system, its privileged methods and subjects, the effect on it of external circumstances, whether political, economic, or social, is a topic for an entire study, a topic at which the present remarks, I am

[3] The issue of the graduate curriculum in classical studies needs urgent study. For a view of the argument over the fit mix of theory and more traditional philological training, see Culler 1981: 210–26.

afraid, can only hint. For our profession, the "sociology of knowledge," as it is called, would investigate not only the knowledge that it develops, teaches, and disseminates, but also other types of knowledge that play a role in its functioning, in particular, "political knowledge" in administration as well as "commonsense" knowledge and what might be called the "knowledge of the Other and the We" (Gurvitch 1971: 63). Such a study would surely find that knowledge as conceived and taught in the profession, as generally in the universities where it is lodged, remains partly esoteric, hermetic, and traditional, and that, paradoxically, the very institutions expected to stimulate and advance these important types of knowledge often arrest their progress and retard or limit their diffusion, quite without any deliberate intention, but simply by the institutions' very functioning. We might also find in the profession something analogous to what Georges Gurvitch (1971: 64) points out about the larger context of universities, namely that, if we consider the other types of knowledge involved in their internal life, such as political and commonsense knowledge, we note that they rarely correspond to the level of the knowledge being taught, and that "the professors who are rightly considered to be the most eminent scholars are not necessarily those whose authority is dominant . . . when questions of administration are under consideration." This would suggest that there is always likely to be a cautious attitude toward innovation in institutions devoted to knowledge in which the conceptual, the symbolic, the collective, and the rational predominate.

The question would still remain, however, as to why the Classics profession gives the appearance of being the most conservative group in a constitutionally conservative institution—conservative in a way that for some observers would sufficiently explain the otherwise curious survival of Classics against the assaults of budgetary stringency in academic institutions, despite the premium these institutions and their supporting culture place, at least in their public rhetoric, on "relevance." It might be argued that by resist-

> Sound humanism does not begin with oneself, but puts the
> world before life, life before man, and respect for others be-
> fore self-interest. (1978: 508)

> Starting from ethnographic experience, I have always aimed
> at drawing up an inventory of mental patterns, to reduce ap-
> parently arbitrary data to some kind of order, and to attain
> a level at which a kind of necessity becomes apparent, un-
> derlying the illusion of liberty. . . . If it were possible to
> prove . . . that the apparent arbitrariness of the mind, its
> supposed spontaneous flow of inspiration, and its seemingly
> uncontrolled inventiveness imply the existence of laws oper-
> ating at a deeper level, we would inevitably be forced to con-
> clude that when the mind is left to commune with itself and
> no longer has to come to terms with objects, it is in a sense
> reduced to imitating itself as object; and that since the laws
> governing its operation are not fundamentally different
> from those it exhibits in its other functions, it shows itself to
> be of the nature of a thing among things. (1969: 10)

Parenthetically, we should note that along with the disso-
lution of the subject and of humanism goes a pair of critical terms dear to traditional humanistic literary criticism:
originality and creativity. What, if anything, they could
mean in a structuralist or poststructuralist context would
require radical reexamination (see Peradotto 1979).

If all this were not enough to chill the blood of traditional humanists, there was yet more to be apprehensive
about. When all was said and done, we might well have
seen in Lévi-Strauss's ideas something really not so radical
at all, but just another form of "lost-world" Rousseauvian
romanticism, a tenacious mythic component of liberal academic thought, which views the world of "mythic man" as
one in which every frustrated longing of the West is fulfilled and all its ills expunged. But the grim logic of his
position would be carried a step further by Jacques Derrida, who articulates the uncomfortable implications of a
form of interpretation that "affirms free-play and tries to
pass beyond man and humanism, the name man being the

name of that being who, throughout the history of meta-
physics or of ontotheology . . . has dreamed of full presence, the reassuring foundation, the origin and end of the
game" (Derrida 1970: 264–65). What this "free-play" will
produce in the vacuum of discredited humanistic values
causes even Derrida, the chief architect of deconstructionism, to set himself in the company of those who "turn their
eyes away in the face of the as yet unnameable which is
proclaiming itself and which can do so, as is necessary
whenever a birth is in the offing, only under the species of
the non-species, in the formless, mute, infant and terrify-
ing form of monstrosity (ibid.).

If classicists were to be faulted for turning their backs
on a dialogue so fearfully oriented, how much more their
colleagues in other disciplines who, with perilous detach-
ment in their engagement with it, appeared to be uncon-
cerned about its disruptive effect on education and society.
Furthermore, unless I am being too generous in my judgment, some of the more sober minds in classical studies
may have divined that structuralism and kindred movements, within classical ranks and without, was becoming *interpretation*, not on its own momentum, but with concepts
derived from psychoanalysis and Marxism or old New
Criticism, with the reinsertion, sometimes subtle, sometimes not so subtle, of the "world" and of "history" into
what was supposed to be a system sealed off from "world"
and "history," constituted of differences and oppositions
independent of the observer (Sheridan 1980: 203). So
handled, structuralism gave all the appearance, at worst,
of irresponsible trifling, and at best, of a fashionable overlay for existing critical practice.

The task still remains in the discipline of overcoming
this resistance to the study of structure, of code, of *langue*
in Saussure's terminology. The humanism and historicism
that the discipline cultivates, not simply as points of pride,
but as defining and inalienable characteristics, need not
necessarily be sacrificed to the study of an ahistorical, synchronic system, which is unintended, virtual, anonymous,

compulsory, unconscious. Many classicists give the impression of believing that such a study necessarily denies the efficacy or value of what they have traditionally given pride of place, what Saussure calls *parole*: concrete, actual, conscious, intended, individual, literary utterance. These sceptics have not been easy to convince that there is something incomplete about a study of intentional language that is not preceded by an analysis of function and system. They are more readily persuaded by Hirsch to make author's intended meaning the norm of correctness in interpretation. But intention seeks means, means have to do with function, and function has to do with system. The analysis of what one wished to do with a thing must start, therefore, with an inventory of its virtual uses and limitations. The analysis of system, or the synchronic approach, is logically prior to a diachronic approach because systems are more intelligible than changes. Careful attention to system will, for example, keep us from assuming that what an author *effects* is necessarily what he *intends*. For he may misuse language against his designs. And, since language at the level of *langue* is exuberant, he may effect far more than his limited intention.

What is more, the literary artifact, insofar as it survives its original historical conditions, leads an unintended existence in an unpredictably altered state of its own language and other literary materials (images, symbols, narrative effects, etc.). Poetic discourse—perhaps all discourse—has no privileged single meaning, but is polysemous. It deliberately exploits the radical ambiguity that lurks as a potentiality at the heart of all discourse. In short, it is the analysis of language insofar as it transcends an individual user's control, whether as prior impersonal code or as subsequent, surviving polysemous text, which needs to find a more comfortable place in contemporary classical studies, but which meets formidable obstacles in certain of the discipline's entrenched positions.

What are these positions? Let me name the more significant among them.

1. The discipline's view of language as mere instrument, constituted wholly by an autonomous subject, in no sense constituting that subject.
2. Its epistemologically naive realism, coupled with a view of language as a representation of things, not as a "closed" system, in which the meaning of a word results from its opposition to other lexical units within the system, with no uncontested relations to external, nonsemiotic reality.[5]
3. Its deep suspicion of "unconscious meaning," of meaning thought to underlie the literal one, and of the iconoclasm presumed to infect all hermeneutics and to demolish our conscious, unreflective, conventional view of reality the way that Marx, Nietzsche, and Freud exhort us to do.
4. Its further suspicion of the presumed impoverishment of meaning resulting from structural and semiotic approaches.
5. Its belief in an "objective" interpretation of the past, "achieved only by exclusive reliance on 'evidence,' unaware that in classics, as in life, the significance of isolated phenomena is accessible only to a unified interpretative vision which must have some positive source outside the phenom-

---

[5] Roland Barthes (1974: 7) has expressed the difference between the philological and the semiotic perspectives in terms of their respective attitudes to linguistic connotation: "Connotation has not had a good press. Some (the philologists, let us say), declaring every text to be univocal, possessing a true, canonical meaning, banish the simultaneous, secondary meaning to the void of critical lucubrations. On the other hand, others (the semiologists, let us say) contest the hierarchy of denotated and connotated; language, they say, the raw material of denotation, with its dictionary and its syntax, is a system like any other; there is no reason to make this system the privileged one, to make it the locus and the norm of a primary, original meaning, the scale for all associated meanings; if we base denotation on truth, on objectivity, on law, it is because we are still in awe of the prestige of linguistics, which, until today, has been reducing language to the sentence and its lexical and syntactical components; now the endeavor of this hierarchy is a serious one; it is to return to the closure of Western discourse (scientific, critical, or philosophical), to its centralized organization, to arrange all the meanings of a text in a circle around the hearth of denotation (the hearth: center, guardian, refuge, light of truth)."

ena themselves."[6]—anything else being an *unconscious* importation of one's own presuppositions and prejudices.

6. The myth of "disinterested scholarship," in contrast to the view expressed by the anthropologist Rodney Needham, when he declares that "no humane discipline, however rigorous, should fail to evoke from students some sharp sense of the quandary of existence, and if it does not do this it is trivial scholarship and morally insignificant" (1983: 3).

As tempting as it is to demonstrate the reality and power of these positions, and to explore their causes, such tasks would carry us into a book-length study of their own. Before passing on, however, we should look more closely at the second position above, the epistemology of naive (or direct) realism, for in my judgment it is the single most damaging obstacle to fruitful theoretical dialogue. It is also the least easy to recognize as something open to question, for it conspires with the innocent prejudices of the "ordinary" man or, more precisely, the encoded forms of folk knowledge dominant in "Standard Average European," and perhaps in all Indo-European language and thought.[7] In this view, "reality," the "world," is composed of more or less stable substances, "things," which are given more or less directly to awareness, predominantly visual. Language, when it is "true to" this direct perception, represents, literally re-presents, things pretty much as they are in themselves. Heraclitean and similar (e.g., postmodern) readings of the world are accordingly dismissed as aberrant, questioning, as they do, not only the priority of "substances" over "accidents," "qualities," "attributes," "relations," "actions," "events," but the very ontological status of "substances." Such questioning seems easy to discredit, for

[6] Silk and Stern (1981: 99), paraphrasing a portion of *Afterphilologie*, Erwin Rohde's defense (1872) of Nietzsche's *Birth of Tragedy* against Wilamowitz.

[7] The term "standard average European" is Whorf's. See Tyler 1987: 149–50.

it flies in the face of everyday experience. It also seems to fail in consistency and clarity, to fall into oxymoron and paradox, doomed as it is to express itself in a language that collaborates with the realist position because it is the chief means whereby it is maintained and disseminated. Your realist man-in-the-street knows in his heart that you *can* walk into the same river twice. He knows this because that's what he *sees*. He also knows in his heart that, grammatically speaking, nouns (substantives) are more real than verbs, because nouns stand by themselves, while verbs are predicated of nouns, mirroring the fact that substances are what "stand under" (Aristotelian ὑποκείμενα) changes, actions, appearances, while actions must be actions *of* something. He knows this because that's what he *sees*. Stephen Tyler (1987: 149–50) offers a tidy summary of this way of looking at the world and of what it implies:

1. *Things*, both as fact and concept, are hegemonic in Standard Average European (SAE) language and thought.

2. The hegemony of things entails the hegemony of the visual as a means of knowing/thinking. *Seeing* is a privileged sensorial mode and a key metaphor in SAE.

3. The hegemony of the visual, among other things: (a) necessitates a reductive ontological correlation between the visual and the verbal; (b) creates a predisposition to think of thinking/knowing as seeing; (c) promotes the notions that structure and process are fundamentally different and that the latter, which is only sequentiality, can always be reduced to the former, which is simultaneity, and thus being dominates becoming, actuality dominates possibility.

4. The hegemony of the visual, of this way of seeing things, is not universal, for it (a) has a history as a commonsense concept in Indo-European, influenced particularly by literacy; (b) is not "substantiated" in the conceptual "structures" of other languages; and (c) is based on a profound misunderstanding of the evolution and functioning of the human sensorium.

ies, written along Foucault's line, would provide the only proper response to the questions I began by asking. This would not be a book like Sandys's or Wilamowitz's or Pfeiffer's *History of Classical Scholarship*, but an "archaeology of classical philology," matching Foucault's "archaeology of the human sciences" (his subtitle for *Les mots et les choses*)—an analysis of the rules of formation that determine the conditions of possibility for all that can be said within the discourse of a particular discipline at any given time. What Foucault purports to do is to present three types of knowledge—the knowledge of living beings (natural history/biology), the knowledge of the laws of language (general grammar/philology), and the knowledge of economic facts (analysis of wealth/political economics), in relation to philosophical and epistemological discourse that was contemporary with them, during a period extending from the seventeenth to the nineteenth century. What Foucault is after is a "positive unconscious" of knowledge, "a level that eludes the consciousness of the scientist and yet is part of scientific discourse." "Unknown to themselves," Foucault claims, "the naturalists, economists, and grammarians [of the period in question] employed the same rules to define the objects proper to their own study, to form their concepts, to build their theories. It is these rules of formation, which were never formulated in their own right, but are to be found only in widely differing theories, concepts, and objects of study, that I have tried to reveal, by isolating, as their specific locus, a level that I have called, somewhat arbitrarily perhaps, archaeological" (1970: xi). Foucault's focus of attention is the so-called Classical period beginning in the mid-seventeenth century and terminating with the eighteenth century, but this analysis is framed by his description of what he terms the underlying *episteme* of the Renaissance on the far side, as of the modern period on the near side, beginning, for Foucault, somewhere between 1790 and 1810 and lasting until 1950. The date 1950 is significant: just as the epistemic configurations of the Classical period were inaccessible to analysis until they began to crumble and yield to new ones, so, Foucault believes, we are able to analyze our own epistemic presuppositions because "the archaeological ground is once more moving under our feet" (1970: xxiv).

Briefly stated—too briefly for a thesis as complex as Foucault's—and limited here to the knowledge associated with language, this is how he characterizes the epistemic configurations of each of these periods.[8] The Renaissance is seen as ruled by the role of resemblance in constructing and organizing knowledge. As Foucault puts it (1970: 17),

> it was resemblance that largely guided exegesis and the interpretation of texts: it was resemblance that organized the play of symbols, made possible knowledge of things visible and invisible, and controlled the art of representing them. The universe was folded in upon itself: the earth echoing the sky, faces seeing themselves reflected in the stars, and plants holding within their stems the secrets that were of use to man. Painting imitated space. And representation—whether in the service of pleasure or of knowledge—was posited as a form of repetition: the theatre of life or the mirror of nature, that was the claim made by all language, its manner of declaring its existence and of formulating its right of speech.

This system of resemblances was thought of as inscribed in the universe itself in the form of signs requiring decipherment or interpretation, whether these came from the observation of natural phenomena, magical practices, sacred scripture, or the writings of Greek and Roman antiquity. Foucault cites a Renaissance naturalist's treatise as an example of this consubstantial quality of knowledge. In Aldrovandi's *Historia serpentum et draconum*, the chapter "On

---

[8] In my reading of *The Order of Things* (as well as of Foucault's other works) I am heavily indebted to Alan Sheridan for the guidance he provides in his *Michel Foucault: The Will to Truth* (1980). (Sheridan is the English translator of *Les mots et les choses* and of other works of Foucault.) I have not found it easy to improve upon his clear and economical summaries of Foucault's dense exposition, which, here and there, I follow verbatim.

the Serpent in General" is arranged under the following headings: equivocation (which means the various meanings of the word *serpent*), synonyms and etymologies, differences, form and description, anatomy, nature and habits, temperament, coitus and generation, voice, movements, places, diet, physiognomy, antipathy, sympathy, modes of capture, death and wounds caused by the serpent, modes and signs of poisoning, remedies, epithets, denominations, prodigies and presages, monsters, mythology, gods to which it is dedicated, fables, allegories and mysteries, hieroglyphics, emblems and symbols, proverbs, coinage, miracles, riddles, devices, heraldic signs, historical facts, dreams, simulacra and statues, use in human diet, use in medicine, and miscellaneous uses (Foucault 1970: 39).

Such a system of signs was understood essentially as the Stoics had expressed it, namely as a triune figure containing the signifier, the signified, and the "conjuction" of resemblance that joined them together (to which, incidentally, Foucault improperly applies the Stoic term τυγχάνον). Language is not conceived as a totality of independent signs but rather as "an opaque mysterious thing . . . which combines here and there with the forms of the world and becomes interwoven with them: so much so that all these elements, taken together, form a network of marks in which each of them may play, in relation to all of the others, the role of content or of sign, that of secret or of indicator" (Foucault 1970: 34)—"an unbroken tissue of words and signs, of accounts and characters, of discourse and forms" (ibid.: 40). We should note in passing that classical scholarship during this period largely takes the form of the collection and reproduction of past notes, virtually free of what we would call criticism, textual or literary (see Pfeiffer 1968–76: 2.143).

In the seventeenth century, the arrangement of signs becomes, in Foucault's view, binary, constituted by signifier and signified, but the link between them, which in the Renaissance had been real even if hidden, is now considered arbitrary, a matter of *representation* rather than of resemblance. The world is no longer itself a language; language itself is separated from the world; and resemblance, once the source and guarantor of knowledge, becomes in the seventeenth century an occasion for error, a charming but unenlightened hodgepodge not yet arrived in the age of reason, of measurement, of order, of newly established empirical fields. The question of the sign's arbitrary relation to the object represented is raised, along with the question of its separation from its presumed natural origin in spontaneous cries emitted by primitive man. A theory of derivation emerges to take account of two things: (1) the capacity of words to migrate from their original significance (the most obvious form of which is thought to be onomatopoeia), and (2) their capacity to expand or contract meaning, to shift sounds, and even to disappear altogether (Sheridan 1980: 56).

The end of this Classical age coincides with the decline of representation and the characterization of all empirical knowledge as an ordering of things by means of signs based upon identity and difference. This ordering governed the theories of language, of living beings, and of the exchange of wealth. What transforms the foundations of knowledge at the end of the eighteenth century as profoundly as they had been transformed at the outset of the Classical age? It is the concept of *History*. What the notion of Order was to Classical thought, History becomes for modern thought: History, not in the sense of mere description of events, but as the fundamental arrangements of knowledge, involving notions of time, of development, of becoming, common to all the empirical sciences that arose at the end of the eighteenth century. The world is now seen to be composed not of isolated elements related by identity and difference, but of organic structures, of internal relations between elements whose totality performs a function. This notion of function gives time a critical role, and in that it diverges dramatically from Classical thought, for which time was conceived only as intervening from the outside in otherwise timeless structures. Observe how Foucault describes this new dimension (1970: 219):

> History . . . becomes divided, in accordance with an ambiguity that is probably impossible to control, into an empirical science of events and that radical mode of being that prescribes their destiny to all empirical beings, to those particular beings that we are. . . . In the nineteenth century, philosophy was to reside in the gap between history and History. . . . It will be Metaphysics, therefore, but only insofar as it is Memory, and it will necessarily lead back to the question of knowing what it means for thought to have a history. This question was to bear down on philosophy, heavily and tirelessly, from Hegel to Nietzsche and beyond.

In the study of language, the controlling concept in the transformation from analysis of general grammar to the new philology was inflection. This notion was not new; until the end of the eighteenth century, inflectional modifications were seen as a representational mechanism (for example, the letters *m*, *s*, *t*, in the endings of the Latin verb were considered to represent the first, second, and third persons, respectively). With the collapse of representation, however, inflection becomes evidence in a new view of languages as no longer a single unchanging entity, but as a plurality of "living, changing organisms possessed of a history, a dark, internal structure" (Sheridan 1980: 67). In this view, the meaning of a word derives from the particular history that determines its formation and alteration in the course of time and its function as one element of a complicated structure. Having lost its primal function as the medium in which signs originate and things can be known, language is seen as folding in upon itself, becoming one object of knowledge among others. But as the necessary medium of scientific discourse, it seemed to require purging of all its alien, subjective elements, of individual will and energy, to become free of error, uncertainty, and supposition. Alongside this quest for linguistic objectivity came the search for a metalanguage independent of natural languages, a pure, symbolic logic (ibid.: 75). Language, having thus lost its classical transparency, returned to the mysterious density it enjoyed in the Renaissance, but now with no intimate connection to reality; it became once again a problem, a barrier, demanding interpretation and exegesis. "The first book of *Das Kapital*," Foucault says (1970: 298),

> is an exegesis of "value"; all Nietzsche is an exegesis of a few Greek words; Freud, the exegesis of all those unspoken phrases that support and at the same time undermine our apparent discourse, our phantasies, our dreams, our bodies. Philology, as the analysis of what is said in the depths of discourse, has become the modern form of criticism. Where, at the end of the eighteenth century, it was a matter of fixing the frontiers of knowledge, it will now be one of seeking to destroy syntax, to shatter tyrannical modes of speech, to turn words around in order to perceive all that is being said through them and despite them.

In a nutshell, language reacquires its density, engendering two projects: one, the attempt to overcome that density (the scientific enterprise); and the other, the attempt to explore it (philology, interpretation, criticism). At the same time, the very notion of "literature" is born, or at least a radically new realization of what it is. "Literature," says Foucault, "is the contestation of philology (of which it is nevertheless the twin figure): it leads language back from grammar to the naked power of speech, and there it encounters the untamed, imperious being of words." In the nineteenth century, and particularly from the Romantics on, literature, says Foucault, "becomes detached from all the values that were able to keep it in general circulation during the Classical age (taste, pleasure, naturalness, truth), and creates within its own space everything that will ensure a ludic denial of them (the scandalous, the ugly, the impossible); it breaks with the whole definition of *genres* as forms adapted to an order of representations, and becomes merely a manifestation of a language which has no other law than that of affirming—in opposition to all other forms of discourse—its own precipitous existence" (1970: 300).

It is important to note that it was Nietzsche, a classical philologist, who first explicitly associated the task of philosophy with a radical reflection on language. To him, and behind him to the rearrangement of knowledge in the collapse of representation a century and a half ago, we owe our ineradicable preoccupation with language, forcing such questions as:

> What is language? What is a sign? What is unspoken in the world, in our gestures, in the whole enigmatic heraldry of our behavior, our dreams, our sicknesses—does all that speak, and if so in what language and in obedience to what grammar? Is everything significant, and, if not, what is, and for whom, and in accordance with what rules? What relation is there between language and being, and is it really to being that language is always addressed—at least language that speaks truly? What, then, is this language that says nothing, is never silent, and is called "literature"? (Foucault 1970: 306)

This is the background against which a radical rewriting of the history of classical philology is called for. Only then, if at all, shall we be in a position to understand what has shaped classical studies fairly consistently by opposition to the great changes in epistemic suppositions that have occurred since the Classical age, and that hardly seem reversible. The philosophical questions about language and about interpretation that come at the end of that process can be ignored only by massive repression or gross cynicism. My discussion began with some fairly sweeping, tentative, largely impressionistic remarks on the absence of the Classics profession from the interdisciplinary forum in which these questions are openly addressed. Would a close reading of the history of classical studies after Foucault's model support a hypothesis that sees our field as operating with the *episteme* of his Classical age, with a view of language as transparent representation, with a rationalism that would see itself threatened by Nietzsche's invitation to a radical reflection on language, and later by an anthropology that would eventually accumulate empirical evidence calculated to undermine still further a viewpoint claiming its basis in universal reason and starting with the axiom that "the accidental truths of history can never become proofs of the necessary truths of reason" (Lessing, in R. Palmer 1969: 38)? Would our Foucaldian reading of classical scholarship further disclose why, in the nineteenth-century bifurcation of history into empirical description of events on the one side, and on the other side, the epistemological question of what it means for thought to have a history, classical studies, doubtless in large part stimulated by the explosive growth of archaeology, would generally follow the primrose path of unrefracted fact?[9]

Foucault's analysis, incidentally, shows how the epistemic transformation between the Classical age and the modern moves through two distinct stages: the first, an endeavor to fit new concepts to the lingering system of representation; the second, the abandonment of representation altogether. Would it be too distorted a picture to represent classical studies as arrested somewhere between these two stages? That is how the picture appears to me, and if, in the present study, issue is taken, whether explicitly or implicitly, with certain previous readings of the *Odyssey*, it will largely be for the philosophical inefficacy of the representationalist position presupposed by them.

My own attitude toward the relationship between philology and semiotic approaches as well as my justification for emphasizing the semiotic is neatly summed up in some re-

---

[9] Operational metaphors play a large role in determining the persuasive power of discourse within a discipline. In my experience, the metaphor of "deconstruction" has a negative effect, on many classicists at least. I wonder if the metaphor of *refraction* might not be preferable. Until *refracted* (broken up, analyzed), the light without which we cannot see the world is invisible, an unperceived, unconscious medium. But refraction does not *destroy* what it "breaks up."

marks of Frederic Jameson (1972: 132) about new intellectual or theoretical movements. Our approach to any new
theoretical position as a coherent system, he says,

> does not so much involve the testing of theories and hypoth-
> eses as it does the learning of a new language, which we mea-
> sure as we go along by the amount of translation we are able
> to effect out of the older terminology into the new. This is,
> incidentally, what explains the tremendous explosion of in-
> tellectual energies generated by a new system of this kind,
> and may serve, indeed, to define the notion of an intellectual
> movement as well. But only a small fraction of the intellec-
> tual energies thus released result in new theory. The over-
> whelming bulk of work done is simply a tireless process of
> translating all the old into the new terms, of endlessly reviv-
> ing numbed perception and intellectual habit by forcing it
> through a new and unfamiliar intellectual procedure, by ex-
> haustively applying the new intellectual paradigm. When
> new discoveries are made, they result, I think, from the way
> in which the new model enlarges or refocuses corners of re-
> ality which the older terminology had left obscured, or had
> taken for granted.

In short, this view of the results of literary analysis coincides with what Viktor Schlovski, a Russian formalist,
claimed to be the distinguishing feature of literary discourse itself, and indeed of all art: *defamiliarization*, a process that aims at a heightening of active awareness as a
countermeasure to the lethargic torpor and erosion of
meaning that results from habitual usage and perception.

If one wishes a name for the dominant focus of the present study, it must, I suppose, be "narratology" or "narrative analysis." If that helps to locate what I am doing in the
field of the reader's experience, fine; that's what names are
for. But names, as we are going to see, are problematical
and deceptive, and before we are finished, we shall be
fairly obsessed with the problems of nomination. "Narratology" is a deceptively simple name for an incredibly complex subfield, only barely emergent, in the larger field of

semiotics, itself still less than clearly defined. Technically defined, narratology is the study of texts that are referential, that are composed of more than one proposition, and—more important—in which temporality is represented (Ducrot and Todorov 1979: 297). One may distinguish at least two fundamental operations in current narratological discussion: description and theory development. To describe is "to try to obtain, on the basis of certain theoretical premises, a rationalized representation of the object of study, while to present a scientific work [i.e., a theory] is to discuss and transform the theoretical premises themselves, after having experienced the object described" (Todorov 1967: 7). Reading is distinct from both of these operations, though obviously it may be affected by them. In the course of this study of the *Odyssey*, I shall be ranging back and forth among these three operations, not always stopping to identify which of them is in play.[10]

Some people, many of them dear to me, especially those not professionally involved with literature, may wonder what purposes are served by this kind of study. Indeed, for too long a disengaged academic aestheticism, which detached the beautiful from the useful and the good, quietly conspired with a bourgeois view of art as mere entertainment to keep it from being taken seriously, or at best to see that it was tolerated as a luxury or at most as a token of good taste. The close study of narrative strategies may indeed, at first sight, seem like a closet, purely academic exercise. But it is not, and in fact many social scientists are turning to the humanistic study of narrative to enrich a perspective now thought to be too narrowly shaped by quantification. The reason for this is that the study of narrative strategies bears upon the most fundamental manner

---

[10] To those inclined to see this as lack of methodological unity and to take scandal at it, I shall only answer that there is no good reason to be worried by it, as long as no logical incompatibility or inconsistency results. As Terry Eagleton says (1983: 198), "we should celebrate the plurality of critical methods, adopt a tolerantly ecumenical posture and rejoice in our freedom from the tyranny of any single procedure."

in which, as societies and individuals, we define our existence in the world. However much one may dispute the intrinsic ethical nature of narrative or the appropriateness of an ethical appraisal of "fiction," no one will seriously contest the fact that historically, for the overwhelming majority of mankind, the vehicle of their most cherished values, the context in which they shape and from which they derive and through which they sustain and authenticate their definitions of the "world" and of "human nature," has been *narrative*. Not philosophy, not science, but narrative, whether religious or secular, whether in the form of myth or history or literary fiction. Current thinking in moral philosophy is explicitly concerned with this. As two ethical theorists have suggested, "We are given the impression that moral principles offer actual grounds for conduct, while in fact they present abstractions whose significance continues to depend on original narrative contexts" (Burrell and Hauerwas 1976: 90). In short, it is difficult, if not impossible, precisely to distinguish a theory of human action from a theory of narrative; neither is found without the other, at least implicitly. Readers of the *Republic* will recognize that it is precisely Plato's realization of this power of narrative to shape conduct that lies at the heart of his vigorous assault on traditional poetry. And early Greek society is not the only place where it is often difficult to find the lines that divide poet from holy man, seer, and prophet, and where there is something like a cult of divinely inspiring Muses. It is no accident that the greatest storyteller in the *Odyssey*, Odysseus himself, has maternal uncles, sons of the arch-trickster Autolycus, whose powers of song go so far beyond simple persuasion, instruction, or entertainment that they are able to cause the blood in a wound to congeal by their incantations (ἐπαοιδαί, 19.457), a power richly documented in a variety of cultures.[11]

It should now be clear why the semiotic analysis of nar-

[11] See, for example, "The Effectiveness of Symbols," in Lévi-Strauss 1963: 181–201.

rative is important and also why there is in some quarters so much resistance to it. *It makes ideology explicit*; it may even be said to have this as its aim. One useful way of defining ideology is as the confusion of linguistic and narrative reality on the one side with "natural" reality on the other; or better perhaps, the confusion of what is being *referred to* with what *is*. By exposing the mechanics according to which narrative discourse operates, semiotics cannot avoid unmasking the process, to which language is ever open, of making what is merely historical and arbitrary seem natural, of turning the merely accidental into the necessary, and of essentializing the merely contingent. Roland Barthes has been indefatigable in describing this process, as in this passage from *The Fashion System* (1983: 285):

> On the one hand, it seems that all societies deploy tireless activity in order to penetrate the [real with] signification[12] and to constitute strongly and subtly organized semiological systems by converting things into signs, the perceptible into the signifying; and on the other hand, once these systems are constituted (or, more precisely, as they are being constituted), human beings display an equal activity in masking their systematic nature, reconverting the semantic relation into a natural or rational one; therein lies a double process, simultaneously contradictory and complementary: of signification and of rationalization.

Umberto Eco also sees semiotics as designed to unmask this process, for "it reveals," he says, "ways in which the labor of sign production can respect or betray the complexity of such a cultural network, thereby adapting it to (or separating it from) *the human labor of transforming stages of the world*" (1976: 297; emphasis added). He goes on to insist that semiotics, in its double guise as a theory of codes and a theory of sign production, is also a form of social criticism (ibid.: 298). I would put this more directly by sug-

[12] I have edited the Ward/Howard translation slightly to accord more closely with what I take to be Barthes's meaning here. They translate ". . . *pénétrer le réel de signification*" as ". . . penetrate the reality of signification." I have replaced that with ". . . penetrate the real with signification."

gesting that sign production—we are concerned mainly with *narrative* sign production—may constrain or enhance the human enterprise of transforming the world to its own desire and design, or it may sustain and authenticate the interests of one social group to the detriment of another in that enterprise. Semiotics questions the powerful, previously unquestioned assumption that language, particularly narrative language, functions according to principles that are the same as, or even remotely like, those of the phenomenal world, or that literature is a reliable source of information about anything other than its own language (De Man 1982: 11).

In these pages I hope to contribute, in my own small way, to the interpretation of early Greek narrative as the groundwork for the later development of philosophy and some of the most fundamental categories of Western thought. An attempt will be made to show how Homeric poetry represents implicit categories of necessity and chance, of fate and human control, of resignation and desire, of the world itself as a universal nexus of cause and effect, and of the human subject, in strictly narrative terms. Unreflective notions of narrative, especially of oral poetic narrative, suggest that it *represents*—literally *re-presents*—a more or less fixed state of the world, or a fixed, inherited tradition. Such views treat literary narratives as if they were exclusively descriptive history, the storyteller telling the tale as he hears it told, portraying the world as it is unreflectively given. This rules out or at least underestimates the possibility that conceptions of the world, of divine being and behavior, of norms of human conduct, may be shaped primarily in narrative and then taken over into life, not vice versa. This relative freedom to fashion and entertain alternative versions of "the world" can be traced to what Sebeok calls "the extraordinary suppleness of the verbal code," a suppleness that, as he says,

> is a consequence of the dual organization of the verbal code, which makes it feasible for the human mind to model the

world and then, in the fashion of a tinkertoy, to "play around" with this model: to take it apart, then reassemble it in many different novel arrangements. The primary function of language, which I have long called a "behavioral organ," and which Chomsky has lately begun calling a "mental organ" . . ., is thus to model the universe, and, moreover, to reconstruct several putative pasts, fabricate many kinds of possible future worlds, imagine death, create both poetry and science. (Sebeok 1986: 91)

The *Odyssey* shows a highly developed awareness of the poet's sense of his power to control and to tinker with the material "given" to him by his tradition. The most impressive example of this is his character Odysseus's ability to narrate a fictitious world—a made-up world—an ability that is not formally distinguishable from the poet-narrator's own exercise of his craft. Along the same lines, I would suggest that the representation of divine activity, especially in the context of prophecy, may owe more to the narrator's sense of power over his materials than to any other factor. The experience of the poet, positioned above his story, with power to choose among eventualities and outcomes, and by hints and forecasts to control the access of his audience to his privileged perspective and design, offers a ready model or metaphor for representing the gods in a position above history, knowing the future because they have the power to effect it, allowing through prophecy some limited human access to this knowledge, but little real power to change its design. As we are going to see, when the Phaeacian king Alcinous comments on the yet-unfulfilled prophecy of Poseidon's attack upon his people, his remarks sum up the situation of the poet as well as of the god (8.570–71):

τὰ δέ κεν θεὸς ἢ τελέσειεν
ἤ κ᾿ ἀτέλεστ᾿ εἴη, ὥς οἱ φίλον ἔπλετο θυμῷ.

(These things the god may bring to fulfillment or leave unfulfilled, as suits his pleasure.)

Chapter 2

POLYAINOS: MYTH VS. FOLKTALE

> Myths project an ideal personality acting on the
> basis of superego demands, while fairy tales depict
> an ego integration which allows for appropriate
> satisfaction of id desires.
> —Bruno Bettelheim, *The Uses of Enchantment*

> The first storyteller is, and will continue to be, the
> teller of fairy tales. Whenever good counsel was at a
> premium, the fairy tale had it, and where the need
> was greatest, its aid was nearest. This need was the
> need created by the myth. The fairy tale tells us of
> the earliest arrangements that mankind made to
> shake off the nightmare which the myth had placed
> upon its chest.
> —Walter Benjamin, "The Storyteller"

> *DESIRE*: a pychological term, the reality of which
> semiotics, far from denying, views as one of the
> lexicalizations of the modality of wanting. Thus
> semiotic research should involve the development of
> a logic of wanting (parallel to deontic logic), in
> which the terms desire and will would designate the
> variables of wanting, and which would then be
> correlated with more complex semantic structures.
> —A. J. Greimas and J. Courtés, *Semiotics and
> Language: An Analytical Dictionary*

ALCINOUS's expression of the god's options, with which the
last chapter ended, provides the basic, abstract formula for
a type of narrative analysis to be employed in the present
study, especially in this and the following chapter. It is

structural analysis, but not in the sense made famous by Claude Lévi-Strauss.[1] He purports to describe patterns that allegedly underlie the text as it is given, and that are usually reducible to an *a priori* principle of binary opposition. These patterns have little in common with the sequential structure. Rather, the basic narrative units, or what he calls "mythemes," are extracted from the chronological (or "diachronic") order as it stands and are regrouped according to their logical, conceptual, or, as he puts it, "synchronic" interrelations, that is to say, interrelations that are nontemporal and noncausal.[2] This type of organization has been called paradigmatic, borrowing from the notion of paradigm in linguistics.[3] But long before Lévi-Strauss applied himself to the study of narrative, Vladímir Propp, the Russian formalist, published a study of Russian folktales (1928) in which a distinctly different type of analysis—still structural—was used. In this type, the structure or formal organization of a text is described without diverging from the linear, chronological sequence of basic narrative units or mythemes. Thus if a tale is constituted out of a series of events *A* through *Z*, the structure of the tale is delineated in terms of this same sequence. Borrowing from the notion of syntax in linguistic analysis, this type has been called syntagmatic structural analysis. These two types of analysis, as Alan Dundes points out, possess contrasting characteristics, appealing to quite dif-

---

[1] Some of the discussion in this and the following chapter appeared, in a provisional version, in Peradotto 1977.

[2] See Lévi-Strauss's "Structural Study of Myth," in *Structural Anthropology* (1963: 202–28). This is a considerably revised version of an essay that first appeared under the same title in Thomas A. Sebeok, ed., *Myth: A Symposium*, Bibliographical and Special Series of the American Folklore Society, vol. 5 (Bloomington, 1955). The terms "synchronic" and "diachronic" have been preserved for the convenience of those wishing to refer back to Lévi-Strauss's essay, even though linguists familiar with these terms in Saussure have been troubled by their misleading application in Lévi-Strauss's usage.

[3] For a brief general discussion of the two types of narrative analysis, paradigmatic and syntagmatic, see Dundes 1968.

ferent scholarly predispositions: "Generally speaking, the syntagmatic approach tends to be empirical and inductive, and its resultant analyses can be replicated. In contrast, paradigmatic analyses are speculative and deductive, and they are not as easily replicated" (Dundes 1968: xii).

Now there is a clear correspondence between Lévi-Strauss's exclusively paradigmatic analysis of narrative and the subject matter that he addresses. In the Amerindian narratives that appear in his monumental *Mythologiques*, chronology and genealogy are for the most part negligible or nonexistent, both within each tale and in the relation of tale to tale.[4] They seem therefore positively to invite paradigmatic analysis and to promise little yield to syntagmatic analysis. By contrast, in Greek (and for that matter Judaeo-Christian) narrative, genealogical preoccupations are prominent, together with rigid temporal priority and posteriority, and irreversible time. More important for our purposes, prophecy, possibly the most critical element in Greek narrative, seems to establish irreversible sequential and causal continuity—teleology—*as an element of structure*.[5] By contrast, in all 813 of the Amerindian tales studied by Lévi-Strauss, there is not a single prophecy.

Propp's analysis is based upon the concept of "function," understood as "an act of a character defined from the point of view of its significance for the course of the action." He argued that such functions serve as the stable, constant elements in a tale, that their number is limited (Propp himself found thirty-one in the set of Russian folktales he studied), and, what is most important, that their sequence is always identical. What follows is Propp's model for a set of Russian folktales:

$$\alpha \; \beta \; \gamma \; \delta \; \varepsilon \; \zeta \; \eta \; \theta \; A \; B \; C \downarrow D \; E \; F \; G \; \frac{H \; J \; I \; K \downarrow Pr \; Rs \; O \; L}{L \; M \; J \; N \; K \downarrow Pr \; Rs} \; Q \; Ex \; T \; U \; W$$

---

[4] It must, however, be questioned whether and to what extent he or his secondary sources have underplayed whatever temporal elements there may be in them. See Terence Turner 1977.

[5] See Peradotto 1977. For a tentative description of the type of analysis that might be brought to bear on prophecy tales, see Peradotto 1974.

The sequence, as we said, is fixed, each letter standing for a particular subject/function relation, e.g., α = prologue defining initial situation; β = absence of family member(s); γ = interdiction addressed to the hero; δ = transgression of the interdiction; etc. If we pass beyond Propp to search for a more universal model, it is not out of any disdain for the kind of culture-specific study his model embodies. It is rather because the Homeric and other extant archaic narrative materials offer insufficient empirical data for developing a sequential model as detailed and specific as Propp's. In the absence of such data, we can never be sure whether what we have is an *unconscious*, more or less *necessary*, *tradition-enforced* story pattern, of the kind hypothesized by Albert Lord (1960: 165–69), or *deliberate* imitation of one storyteller's pattern by another, or, for comparable sequences within a single narrative, the deliberate choice of a narrator to make them similar.

To concretize this methodological dilemma, let me introduce an example that will serve a larger purpose later on. It has long been recognized that there is a striking resemblance between Menelaus's tale of his encounter with Proteus in *Odyssey* 4 and the story of Odysseus's visit to Tiresias in book 11 (which will in fact be the main focus of our investigation in this chapter). This resemblance has led to claims that the Menelaus tale is an imitation of the Odysseus tale (Focke 1943: 201n.1), or that the latter is an imitation of the former (Kirchhoff 1879: 221; Von der Mühll 1940: c. 723.43; Theiler 1950: 105; 1962: 13), or that both are versions of a traditional and generic configuration, a visit to the land of the dead and the return therefrom (Lord 1960: 168; cf. also Powell 1970). In outline, the Menelaus story goes as follows: on his return voyage from Troy, he is detained on the island of Pharos by adverse winds. There he is encouraged by the goddess Eidothea, who gives him elaborate instructions on how to trap her father, the prophetic, metamorphic sea-god Proteus, in order to ask him why his fleet can get no further. This done, Proteus enjoins upon Menelaus a journey up the Nile

context, whether explicitly (as here in the *Odyssey*) or implicitly (as, for example, in certain of the Platonic dialogues, such as the *Republic*).

(β) The hero has experienced an unseasonably long detour on his journey home. Note how this also implies a larger narrative frame.

(γ) The hero finds himself blocked from continuing his journey home.

(A) The hero gets assistance from a goddess who can only act as an intermediary.

(B) The goddess gives the hero *elaborate* instructions on how to gain access to the prophet.

(C) The hero loses a shipmate before encountering the prophet: the helmsman Phrontis in Menelaus's tale (3.278–83, although note how this element is displaced in the *narration*, as distinct from the *narrative*), and the no-account Elpenor in Odysseus's tale.

(δ) There is mention of wind blowing: Zephyr in Menelaus's tale (4.402), Boreas in Odysseus's (10.507). Worth noting is that in both tales this mention occurs in the goddess's instructions, prior to the event itself.

(ε) There is explicit mention of the passage of time: from day to night to day in Menelaus's tale (4.429–31), from night to day to night in Odysseus's tale (10.541, 11.12–13).

(ζ) There is explicit mention of the kind of light in which the encounter between the hero and the prophet takes place: high noon in Menelaus's tale (4.400), pitch darkness in Odysseus's tale (11.15–19).

(η) The hero awaits the prophet by the edge of a body of water: the seashore in Menelaus's tale, the bank of the river Ocean in Odysseus's tale.

(D) The prophet, even though he already knows it, asks the hero his purpose in coming.

(E) The prophet gives the hero three pieces of information: (a) how the hero is to achieve his return home, including (a¹) what god needs to be propitiated, (a²) at what location, namely at a place to be reached by an inland journey, and (a³) by what means, namely sacrifice; (b) what the situation back home is; and, (c) though wholly unbidden by the hero and without any other motivation in the plot, how the hero's career will end. It should be noted that, unlike Menelaus, Odysseus is *not* informed how to achieve his *first* return home (a), even though that is, after all, the explicit reason for consulting Tiresias. More shall be said about this problem later. For our present purposes, we should observe that the *function* being discussed here—what god needs to be appeased, where, and by what sacrifice—has been displaced from Odysseus's first return to his second.

(F) The hero performs the required journey, terminating it with a sacrifice to propitiate the angry god. Note that in Odysseus's case this function is not explicitly narrated.

(G) The hero returns home. Note again that in Odysseus's case this function is fulfilled with respect to the first return, but not the second. We will have much more to say later about the silence of the text here and at F, as well as the displacement in E.

The similarities here are simply too striking to discount. But we search in vain through Homer and, for that matter, the rest of archaic epos and even the mythographers for a similar pattern. As philologists, blighted with a paucity of data, we have been far hastier than our scientific peers to generalize from too few instances, but even a few more examples of this particular pattern might have encouraged us to infer a tradition or convention. Actually, when we look more closely at these two tales, it is not only the likenesses that are striking, but even more the uniform differences in the midst of these likenesses. Far from having a situation like the one we find in Propp's Russian folktales, we have a pair of nearly identical tales that, at certain points, diverge from one another. Not only do they diverge, but they appear consistently to do so in a way that makes the variants analogous to one another. Let me try to clarify this important observation.

Element A shows us a goddess intermediary who in one

tale is benevolent and freely seeks out the frustrated hero
to assist him, but in the other tale is initially hostile and
must be sought out by the hero, confronted, and threatened before her assistance is given. This difference between Eidothea and Circe is a logical opposition of contra-
riety (or inversion): friendly/hostile. So also is the
difference between the two heroes at this point: passive/
active. Now Propp catalogs statistically significant variations (e.g., there are 23 variations on the general function
labelled "A" and called "villainy"), but he attaches no importance to *kinds* of variation, as, in the case before us, variations that are contraries (or in Propp's usage, inversions)
of one another. For example, in his analysis, an interdict
violated serves the same function as an order obeyed, or
with respect to a function of his (F) closer to the one we
have labelled "A," there is no significant difference between an agent that appears of its own accord, one that is
sought out and seized by the hero (these two being contraries), or one that is discovered accidentally by him. And
indeed, if we had no more variation than that involving
Eidothea/Circe and Menelaus/Odysseus in our two stories,
we would probably have to consider it insignificant.

But when we look at other points of divergence, even
those which seem extremely incidental to the core of the
plot (δ, ε, ζ), we find that they are analogous or homologous with the Eidothea/Circe pair. In other words, the elements in each of these other pairs of variants are related
to one another as Eidothea (+) is logically related to Circe
(−), i.e., as contraries.

    (A) Eidothea (+): Circe (−).
    (C) Phrontis (+): Elpenor (−). The characterization of
        Phrontis (. . . ὃς ἐκαίνετο φῦλ' ἀνθρώπων / νῆα κυβερ-
        νῆσαι, 3.282–83) indicates that he is the *best* at what he
        does, while Elpenor is the *worst*, lacking in both military
        and mental power (. . . οὔτε τι λίην / ἄλκιμος ἐν πολέμῳ
        οὔτε φρεσὶν ᾗσιν ἀρηρώς, 10.552–53); and the meanings
        of their names—"Thoughtful, son of Benefactor" (+) /

"Illusion-man" (−)—match the descriptions of their characters. The characterization of Elpenor's wits even provides an *explicit negation* of Phrontis's significant name: οὔτε φρεσὶν ἦσιν ἀρηρώς.

(δ) Zephyr (+): Boreas (−).

(ε) Night to day (+): day to night (−).

(ζ) High noon (+): pitch darkness (−).

(D) Proteus (+): Tiresias (−). The difference here has nothing to do with the narrative function of the prophets, but with their characterizations: the one is immortal, volatile, metamorphic, reluctant; the other dead, sluggish, unreluctant.

(E[c]) Menelaus is destined for immortality (+), Odysseus for death (−).

Our initial purpose in introducing this example was to illustrate a case in which remarkable and minute structural similarities are evident, but which, because we have only two instances, give us no grounds for inferring a traditional rule of invariance of the kind discovered by Propp in the Russian material. In the course of our investigation, however, we have noticed something not found in the Proppian material. There is a consistent homology at each point of divergence within a larger framework of structural identity, and this cannot be accidental; not necessarily deliberate or even conscious, but certainly not accidental. If, for the sake of argument, we were to consider the structural identity a traditional invariable, then we would also consider the points of divergence substitutional (or paradigmatic) sets. Their relation to one another is logical and comparative rather than causal, more like the relation of elements in lyric poetry than those in the plot line of narrative. None of them except the last—the ultimate fate of the hero—is essential to the linear, syntagmatic, causal sequence of the narrative. Understood in terms of Propp's definition of *function*, none of them has "significance for the course of the action." They could, in other words, be removed without damaging the plot line. Their effect, as metaphoric mirrors of the narrative endings, seems to be to reinforce and focus attention on the difference in those endings. That is to say, they are motivated from *outside* the narrative. And we will soon see that this can also be said of the endings themselves.

The complexity of this situation is nowhere matched in the Russian narratives out of which Propp developed his model. That is the main reason why we must look beyond such a model. There have been analytic theories since Propp's that have sought both to reduce the number of his functions and to construct a more universal model, one, in other words, that would fit not only a small subset of culture-specific narratives (Russian folktales), but any narrative whatever. The most fruitful of these attempts has been that by Claude Bremond. His more economical model opens up the theoretical alternatives closed down by the actual, culture-specific choices that make up the Russian folktale and substitutes a universal map of possible itineraries for Propp's fixed and frozen linearity (see Ricoeur 1985: 39). In order for anything at all to be narrated, Bremond argues (1973: 131–32), it is both a necessary and a sufficient condition that it pass through three phases: (1) a situation containing some potentiality (some lack to be liquidated, some desire to be fulfilled); (2) the actualization of that potentiality; (3) the conclusion of this action. In this sequence, each successive phase logically implies its antecedent; there can be no achievement or conclusion without actualization, nor any actualization without potentiality. On the other hand, no phase logically implies its successor; at each of these moments an alternative is opened up: potentiality can evolve into transition to actualization or remain potentiality; transition to actualization can reach fulfillment or fail to do so (see Fig. 1). Note the correspondence between this abstract formulation and Alcinous's remark about his father's prophecy to which we have referred (8.570–71). The formulation also conforms to the speculations of Valery (1957: 1467) about a literary work

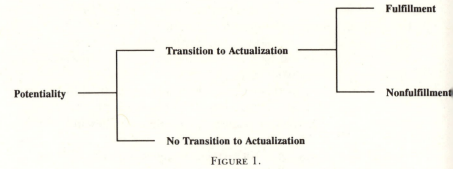

<figure>FIGURE 1.</figure>

that, instead of disguising its options at each successive
stage, would reveal them:

> Peut-être serait-il intéressant de faire une fois une oeuvre
> qui montrerait à chacun de ses noeuds la diversité qui s'y
> peut présenter à l'esprit, et parmi laquelle il *choisit* la suit
> unique qui sera donnée dans le texte. Ce serait là substituer
> à l'illusion d'une détermination unique et imitatrice du réel,
> celle du *possible-à-chaque-instant*, qui me semble plus véritable.

> (It might perhaps be of interest for once to make a literary
> work which would show at each of its junctures the variety
> which is available to the mind, and amidst which it *makes a
> choice of* that single sequence which will be given in the text.
> This would be to take the illusion of a determination which
> has no options and which copies reality, and to substitute for
> it the illusion of the *"possible-at-each-moment,"* which for me
> shows more verisimilitude.)

In the quest for assurance that a universal model has
been achieved, a still more severe, abstract representation
than Bremond's may be preferred. Some may find it in the
semiotic definition of "narrative program" (*programme nar-
ratif*) by Greimas and Courtés (1982: 245), although it is
not essentially different from Bremond:

> The *narrative program* (abbreviated NP) is an elementary syn-
> tagm of the surface narrative syntax, composed of an utter-

ance of doing governing an utterance of state. It can be represented under the following forms:

NP = F [S1 → (S2 ∪ Ov)]
NP = F [S1 → (S2 ∩ Ov)]
where: F   = function
       S1   = subject of doing
       S2   = subject of state
       O   = object (which can undergo a semantic investment in the form of v : value)
       []   = utterance of doing
       ()   = utterance of state
       →   = function of doing (resulting from the conversion of the transformation)
       ∪∩   = junction (conjunction or disjunction) indicating the state, the consequences of the doing.

It should not escape the notice of classicists how utterly Aristotelian this scheme is, relying as heavily as it does on the concept of teleology. The real beginning of all narrative (or if not of *all* narrative, at least of the large class constituted by Western narrative) is its end.[6] The Aristotelian notion of teleology has been so vigorously assailed by scientists and philosophers that we may be intimidated from using it, even where its virtues seem most obvious—in the study of narrative. Aristotle's remarks on *telos* look almost as if they had been designed as tools for narrative analysis:

> "That for the sake of which" (τὸ οὗ ἕνεκα) is an end (τέλος) for the sake of which other things occur but which does not in turn occur for the sake of anything. (*Meta.* 2. 994b9)

> The initiating principle (ἀρχή) is that for the sake of which a process of becoming takes place, and this is always the "end" or "goal" (τέλος). (*Meta.* 9. 1050a8)

[6] An early version of the remainder of this chapter and the bulk of the next chapter appeared in *Oralità: Cultura, Letteratura, Discorso* (Atti del Convegno Internazionale, Urbino 1980), edited by Bruno Gentili and Giuseppe Paioni (Rome, 1986), pp. 429–59.

"The end justifies the means" could never be truer than in the art of storytelling. Events in a narrative are determined by its end. In the telling, however, a narrative gives us the illusion of being motivated, as a historical account appears to be motivated, from the opposite direction, from beginning to end—event A causing event B, event B causing event C, and so forth, until the conclusion is reached. It is in effect a process of retroactive necessity in composition generating, in performance, the illusion of progressive contingency. Set in slightly different terms—those of Ricoeur (1984: 37)—in ethics, the subject precedes the action, in the order of ethical qualities; in poetics, the composition of the action by the poet governs the ethical quality of the characters. It should be obvious how easily this illusion could both serve ideological purposes and lead to a theory of narrative art as imitation or representation.

Events in a narrative are determined by its end. That should be qualified. There are certainly determinants operating on narrative that come from outside of it altogether—"cultural constraints of credibility" (Ricoeur), if you will, varying in restrictiveness, governing the choice and shape of situations and imposing rules of development conforming to accepted or acceptable notions of truth, probability, necessity, propriety, logic, beauty, nature, etc. This whole category we can call *motivation*, and the canon that restricts it *verisimilitude*.[7] What we are mainly concerned with, however, is that set of determinants *within* the narrative, relationships of logical implication, exclusion, compatibility by which an event B both presupposes an event A, which is prior to it, and makes possible an event C, which is subsequent to it. This category we can call *function*, defined, if we follow Propp, as the significance an event has in the development of the plot, or more precisely if we follow Bremond, the signifi-

[7] On verisimilitude, see *Communications* 11 (1968). This entire issue is devoted to verisimilitude, but see especially Gerard Genette, "Vraisemblance et motivation," 5–21.

cance an event has in relation to some finality, whether it is some proximate, short-term finality or the ultimate finality, the end of the narrative (see Bremond 1973: 131). This distinction between the function and the motivation of a narrative event is crucial. If its function is the purpose it serves in advancing the narrative towards its conclusion, its motivation is that which it finds necessary in dissimulating its function. Motivation is the domination of convention and tradition restricting the way a story may go; function is the internal play transcending or at least circumventing conventionally understood "reality." To use a metaphor derived from economics by Gerard Genette, function is a *profit*, motivation a *cost* (Genette 1968: 20). The most economical and, as an instrument of ideology, the most persuasive narrative units would therefore be those which require no explicit motivation—those, in other words, which offer no obstacle to credibility. In terms of motivation, then, narratives can be classified as follows:[8]

1. *Implicitly motivated narrative*: That which follows the canons of *verisimilitude* closely enough to require no explanation. It appears "right" or "proper" or "natural" to its audience, or, as Aristotle would say, "necessary or probable." Example: *The queen asked for her carriage and went for a ride.*

2. *Explicitly motivated narrative*: (a) Attribution of motive to an *individual*. Example: *The queen asked for her carriage and then went to bed, for she was very capricious.* (b) Attribution of motive to a *class*. Example: *The queen asked for her carriage and then went to bed, for, like all women, she was capricious.*

3. *"Arbitrary" narrative*: that which puzzles its audience or taxes their credibility, requiring but not supplying motivation. Example: *The queen asked for her carriage and then went to bed.*

Formally, nothing separates type 1 from type 3. The difference depends on a judgment that is culturally variable and wholly extrinsic to the text. Depending on time and

[8] This classification and the example are derived from Genette 1968: 21.

place, a class 1 narrative could become a class 3 narrative, and vice versa.

Consider briefly three examples from the *Odyssey*, two of them subjects of more detailed discussion later in this book. The first is the point where, in the cave of the Cyclops, Odysseus is first asked his identity. He does something unusual from the point of view of a verisimilitude inferable from the *Iliad*: instead of naming himself and referring to his own *kleos* or reputation, he lists himself among the anonymous *laoi*, the "troop" or host of Agamemnon. To be sure, on the level of motivation this is a thinly veiled threat to warn the Cyclops that Odysseus has powerful allies. But even in such a context, the suppression of one's own name is unusual. Later on, when Odysseus is pressed to be more specific, he gives a fictitious name, calling himself anonymity itself, "Outis," or "Noman," and thus sets up the famous misunderstanding in which blinded Polyphemus, from within the cave, cries out to his neighboring Cyclopes that Noman is doing him harm. Now in neither case has Odysseus been able to foresee or to manage the precise set of circumstances that allows the pun on Outis to work. In retrospect, we see that his anonymity and the choice of that precise name, Outis, is functionally necessary to the pun that saves Odysseus's life, but its motivation in the progress of performance is extremely arbitrary. The effect achieved by the choice of the name Outis is not, as Odysseus claims (9.414), the product of his own cunning *mētis*, but of the poet's. No Odysseus can know his own future, as the poet knows it, and if he cannot, then neither should he be able to pull off the ingenious stunt here achieved. Beyond the intuitive power, the imaginative anticipation of probabilities that is *mētis*, the deed would require a knowledge of the indeterminate and coincidental. It is a remarkable narrative moment where the poet and his hero merge, but so clever is the motivational cover and the witty distraction of its climax that the casual reader or listener will miss the subterfuge. Odysseus's manipulation of Polyphemus is rudimentary compared to the poet's manipulation of his audience here, for their pleasure in the outcome is founded on a substantial deception. It is *mētis* at its best: a story about *mētis*, achieved by *mētis*. The same goes for an action of Polyphemus. The first time he returns to his cave with his flocks, he acts presumably as any herdsman would and segregates the females and their young from the males, which are left in the yard outside the cave. The second time, however, he does something unusual: he brings the males inside the cave, because, we are told, "he suspected something or else because some god had so directed him" (9.339):

ἤ τι ὀϊσάμενος, ἤ καὶ θεὸς ὣς ἐκέλευσεν.

In retrospect, we see that the presence of the males is functionally necessary to the escape of Odysseus and his men under their bellies, but its motivation is patently hurried and comparatively weak. And verisimilitude is circumvented or suspended, as so often in the *Odyssey*, by the poet's activity posing as divine activity.

The third example is drawn from book 23, where Penelope's misgivings about Odysseus's identity are finally laid aside as he recounts the "unapparent signs" (σήματα κεκρυμμένα, 23.110), the unique secret of their bed's construction. The incident functions to permit Penelope cleverly to test Odysseus as he had tested her and to resolve any lingering uncertainty about who and what kind of man has returned. This is why the poet makes Odysseus construct so singular and strange a bed, one of its posts an ancient olive trunk rooted in the earth. But Odysseus's own reason for constructing it is a motivation gap to be filled in by audience/readers, if they are not in fact charmed away from it by the rich overlay of detail in the artificer's description.

As we have said, then, the function of every event in the narrative is ultimately determined by the end. But the end itself is determined from outside the narrative.[9] One for-

---

[9] This should be qualified. The relationship of influence between what

mulation of this external determination of the end are the terms "tragic" and "comic." A more abstract formulation, sticking ever close to Bremond's universal model, would be to speak of the nonachievement (or frustration) of desire or its achievement. Although these two types do not differ essentially as narrative structures, the one tends to stress the mortality and relative impotence of the human subject in the face of what might be termed most generally *consistent external resistance*—the will of the gods, "fate," "the way things are," laws of nature inferred from experience, the incommensurability of the world, the inevitability of death. The other represents an optimistic, wish-fulfilling emancipation from this external resistance, born of human desire. In short, one is a story in which mainly things happen to the human subject; the other is a story in which mainly that subject acts.

The first is akin to what Aristotle described as the best kind of plot, that, namely, which proceeds through necessity or high probability to a tragic conclusion; by contrast, the second is organized so as to include a higher incidence of chance and accident (still to speak in Aristotelian terms) and to conclude happily with the achievement of desire. In moral terms, the first type tends to equate justice with the will of the gods or the ineluctable "way" of nature; the second tends toward something like an absolute correlation between happiness or suffering and moral desert,[10] the ideal desideratum of culture. This second type locates man as active subject and agent in a world that is more or less

───

happens in narrative and what happens in extranarrative "reality" is not simple, and is better characterized as dialectical or reciprocal, rather than as unidirectional. What I mean to suggest here is that the end of *a particular narrative* is determined from outside *that narrative*, even though that "outside" influence may be another or other narratives, or something itself conditioned by narrative. Furthermore, I would not wish to give the impression that the desperate problematic of what is "inside" a text and what is "outside" of it is being ignored. (On this last point, see Goldhill 1984.)

[10] Sometimes conveyed in verbal formulas like ἐοικότι . . . ὀλέθρῳ (*Od.* 1.46).

tractable to human design, desire, and work, and that en-
courages him to cultivate hope (Homeric ἔλπις, ἐέλδωρ,
ἐλπώρη). The first type locates him as passive object in a
world that is inflexibly resistant to control by his knowledge or his power, and that enjoins him to cultivate endurance (Homeric τλημοσύνη).

The narrative of desire accomplished and the narrative
of desire frustrated are abstract analytic models, but I
would argue (though I shall not do so here) that they bear
a close correspondence empirically to traditional narrative
types referred to as *Märchen* (or folktale) and myth respectively, at least in the European context. So I will be using
these terms rather than the cumbersome terminology
"narrative of desire accomplished" and "narrative of desire frustrated."[11] The ending of myth, insofar as human

[11] On the nature and structure of *Märchen* and its relation to myth and
heroic legend, see especially Bascom 1965; de Vries 1954, 1958, 1961;
Honti 1931; Jolles 1956; Lüthi 1964, 1970; Röhrich 1956; Thompson
1946; von der Leyen 1958, 1959; and von Beit 1952–57, 1965. For the
psychological ramifications in the contrast between myth and *Märchen*,
see Bettelheim 1976; Bühler 1958; Otto Rank 1919; and Róheim 1941.
Bettelheim expresses the narrative differences between myth and *Märchen* in psychoanalytic terms: "Myths project an ideal personality acting
on the basis of superego demands, while fairy tales depict an ego integra-
tion which allows for appropriate satisfaction of id desires" (1976: 41).

The correspondence between my abstract analytic models and historical traditional tales, at least in the European context, is, I believe, defen-
sible, although space limitations prevent us from pursuing its demonstra-
tion here. Achieving uniformity, to say nothing of universality, in
definition of narrative types, especially of "myth," is a difficult task,
fraught with controversy. This leads Page, in *Folktales in Homer's Odyssey*,
where we might expect a definition of folktale, or at least a discussion of
the problems of definition, to say "I should prefer to shirk the task of
defining precisely what I mean my 'folktale' " (1972: 117). Kirk (1970:
31–41) does much better with the distinction between folktale and myth,
though I would argue that he appears to miss the ideological social function of folktale by reducing its role almost exclusively to "entertainment,"
without asking why it is that the mind is "entertained" or pleased by this
or that element or formal feature rather than another. Categorizing tales
will vary depending upon the relative importance one attaches to formal
features, social function, power of principal characters, performative

agents are concerned, generally concentrates on the extreme form of human loss, the completely predictable and
necessary, and the absolute conclusion of anyone's story,
death. The *Märchen* ordinarily ends with the achievement
of desire, usually a very concrete desire, for example, sexual or economic: the beautiful princess or handsome
prince, the hidden treasure or the pot of gold.

In the interest of clarification, let us move away from the
Greek context for a moment to examine the manner in
which the conclusions of the tales in the *Thousand and One
Nights* are determined by both of these outlooks or voices,
the one dominant, the other subdued. Each tale in the collection tends to end with a variation on a common formula, as in the tale of Sinbad:

> The porter remained a constant visitor at the house of his
> illustrious friend, and the two lived in amity and peace until
> there came to them the spoiler of worldly mansions the Dark
> Steward of the graveyard, the Shadow which dissolves the
> bonds of friendship and ends alike all joys and all sorrows.

The frame-story for the whole collection ends similarly:

> Shahriyar reigned over his subjects in all justice, and lived
> happily with Shahrazad until they were visited by the De-
> stroyer of all earthly pleasures, the Annihilator of men.

The postscript of the narrator, which takes the form of a
prayer to Allah quite obviously shaped under Aristotelian
influence, suggests in explicit form both the analogy between narrative and life implicit in the structure of the

---

context, temporal and spacial setting, sacred or secular attitude of audience, and a host of other aspects. (It should be clear that my working
definitions attach most importance to the first three of these aspects.) For
the problems involved in the more or less standard distinctions between
myth, legend, and folktale, especially from an empirical point of view and
in a non-European context, see especially Ruth Finnegan 1970: 361ff. I
am deeply indebted to Professor Finnegan for her copious and generous
comments on an oral version of the present argument, particularly on the
hazards of seeking universality in defining tale types. I also owe much to
the comments of Dina Sherzer on the same version.

whole work, and the attitude toward time and history that has determined the end of the frame-story and of each of the framed stories: an attitude that enjoins readers to locate themselves as characters in a larger narrative whose unknown conclusion lies in the hands of a divine narrator:

> Now praise and glory be to Him who sits throned in eternity above the shifts of time; who, changing all things, remains Himself unchanged; who alone is the Paragon of all perfection [completeness, being finished]. And blessing and peace be upon His chosen Messenger, the Prince of Apostles, our master Mohammed, to whom we pray for an auspicious END.

This can be represented schematically (see Fig. 2). Just as Shahrazad puts off death by the telling of tales and the constant renewal of sexual desire, but is finally taken by the Annihilator of men and the Destroyer of desire, so too we take pleasure in the story of Shahrazad telling stories— we who are characters in a larger story, doomed to end the way her story ends, and the stories she tells end. Jorge Luis Borges, that imp of the perversely paradoxical, suggests an escape from both death and narrative conclusion—or their infinite deferral—by offering a version of the *Thousand and One Nights* in which Shahrazad, on the 602nd night, tells the story of the *Thousand and One Nights*, thus, Zeno-like, collapsing the whole onto an infinitely divisible center, past which, without discontinuing the narrative, one can never get![12]

.   .   .

The two opposing determinants under discussion are at work in the *Odyssey*, which has been so obviously put together out of a variety of pre-existing tales. The *Odyssey* is the fullest embodiment of Odysseus's epithet πολύαινος

---

[12] Borges, "Partial Magic in the *Quixote*," in *Labyrinths: Selected Stories and Other Writings*, trans. and ed. Donald A. Yates and James E. Irby (New York, 1962), 195.

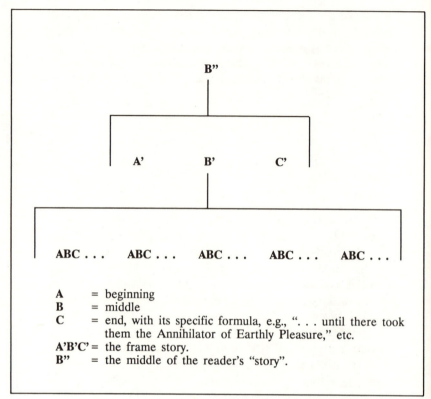

FIGURE 2.

in both the active and the passive senses of that word: "the man about whom many tales (*ainoi*) are told" and "the man who [himself] has many tales to tell." But the multiplicity of these *ainoi*, "tales," reduces ultimately to the two basic possibilities in our model: one, the tale of the master trickster (*polymētis*) and technician (*polymēchanos*) who achieves his purposes in a hostile environment; and the other the tale of one who has little choice other than to endure the full load of the world's resistance (*polytlas*). That way of expressing the oppositions necessitates a clarification in a point that has so far been but lightly touched on. What we are calling "myth" and "*Märchen*" here are not disengaged tale types, nor are they merely abstract analytical models. They are not, in other words, ideologically innocent. They are, or are at least vehicles for, *opinions on the world*. The phrase derives from Mikhail Bakhtin, and it is by reference to his concept of "dialogism" that the basic orientation of our investigation can be explained. The term "dialogism" denotes generally the epistemological mode of opposed and mutually conditioning voices or viewpoints that is found in discourse dominated by "heteroglossia," and the presence of which in the *Odyssey* it is my purpose to articulate.[13] What I have chosen the terms "myth" and "*Märchen*" to designate would, in Bakhtinian terminology, be called respectively "centripetal" and "centrifugal" narrative. By "centripetal" Bakhtin means forces in any language or culture that exert a unifying, centralizing, homogenizing and hierarchizing influence; such forces tend to be closely associated with dominant political power, with the official and heroic, with "high" literary genres and "correct" language. By "centrifugal" he means those forces which exert a disunifying, decentralizing, stratifying, denormatizing influence; these forces tend to be associated with the disempowered, the popular and carnivalesque, with the antics of the trickster, rogue, and outlaw, with "low" literary genres and dialects (1981: 272–73).

Some cultures, discourses, narratives display the collision of the centripetal and centrifugal more openly and

---

[13] In an essay likely to be of great interest to hellenists, "Epic and Novel" (1981: 3–40), Bakhtin argues that among literary genres the novel tends to be the most dialogical, while epic tends to be monological. But readers of Bakhtin have been troubled by this as indeed by his entire attempt to distinguish the novel from the epic. See, for example, Todorov 1984: 80–93. Even Bakhtin himself appears to have found his distinction problematical. "Epic and Novel" was first published in 1970, but it was written in 1941. Twenty years later, he is calling the epic one among several aspects of the novelistic (Todorov 1984: 90). In any case, I would venture to say that close readers of Homer are far more likely to recognize the *Odyssey* in Bakhtin's characterization of the novel than in his account of epic.

comfortably than others, but the centripetal tendency, which Bakhtin considers correlative to all power, favors the creation of what he calls an "authoritative discourse," as opposed to an "internally persuasive discourse." "A word, discourse, language or culture undergoes 'dialogization,' " says one of Bakhtin's editors, "when it becomes relativized, de-privileged, aware of competing definitions for the same things. Undialogized language is authoritative or absolute" (Michael Holquist in Bakhtin 1981: 427). An individual's development, an ideological process in Bakhtin's view, is characterized by a sharp gap between the categories of "authoritative discourse" and "internally persuasive discourse": "in the one," he says,

> the authoritative word (religious, political, moral; the word of a father, of adults and of teachers, etc.) that does not know internal persuasiveness, in the other the internally persuasive word that is denied all privilege, backed up by no authority at all, and is frequently not even acknowledged in society (not by public opinion, nor by scholarly norms, nor by criticism), not even in the legal code. (1981: 342)

"Word" in the quote above (Russian *slovo*), and the *-log-* in Bakhtin's "dialogism" (*dialogizm*) refer, like Greek *logos*, to discourse in the broadest sense, and so signify individual words as well as ways of using words, such as utterances, arguments, narratives, plots (Bakhtin 1981: 427). When I speak of the two "voices" in the *Odyssey*, I mean, like Bakhtin, not only actual instantiations of the narrative structures I am calling *myth* and *Märchen*, but any use of language that belongs to or emerges from the particular opinion on the world sustained by one or the other of these narrative types. Two examples will serve to concretize what is meant here.

The first is in *Odyssey* 5, where Zeus dispatches Hermes to Calypso to order Odysseus's release. Calypso's response lays bare the asymmetry in the norms of sexual conduct governing males and females (118–20):

σχέτλιοί ἐστε, θεοί, ζηλήμονες ἔξοχον ἄλλων,
οἵ τε θεαῖς ἀγάασθε παρ' ἀνδράσιν εὐνάζεσθαι
ἀμφαδίην, ἤν τίς τε φίλον ποιήσετ' ἀκοίτην.

(You gods are unbearable, in your jealousy exceeding others:
you stand aghast at goddesses who openly sleep with men, if
ever one of them wants to make a man her bedmate.)

When we place that statement against the larger backdrop of female sexual conduct and of the "centripetal" social reaction to it and comment on it, not only in the *Odyssey* but indeed also in the rest of archaic epos, it is not easy to conceive how what Calypso is allowed to say could have been placed on the lips of a *human* character. It has already been lent definite if muted prolepsis in this book's opening lines, with the image of the goddess Eos rising up from the side of her mortal lover Tithonus. It can be seen as representing revolt against a system whose order is made to depend on the suppression of female sexual desire in a way that is not expected of males. It would not have appeared at all in a less dialogic text. Even here, it is muted by a narrative environment dominated by the conventional, "centripetal" voice that requires tight constraints on female libido. It is hardly accidental that Calypso's island is made to occupy the center of the sea, distant from all forms of social, political, or religious normativeness, where even the divine crosser of borders is uncomfortable (5.100–102):

τίς δ' ἂν ἑκὼν τοσσόνδε διαδράμοι ἁλμυρὸν ὕδωρ
ἄσπετον; οὐδέ τις ἄγχι βροτῶν πόλις, οἵ τε θεοῖσιν
ἱερά τε ῥέζουσι καὶ ἐξαίτους ἑκατόμβας.

(Who, unless against his will, would make so long a passage
as this over the endless salt sea? Nor is there near at hand
any *polis* of men who make sacrifices and choice hecatombs
to the gods.)

Furthermore, in offering the paradigmatic fates of Orion and Iason to support her charge of divine male jealousy,

Calypso is also made to enunciate the powerful sanction against forbidden conduct. Her revolt ends limply, and as she gives voice to the grand, "centripetal" principle already enunciated by Hermes, "the mind of Zeus is uncircumventable," she is made to suppress, along with her desire, all traces even of her grammatical gender in a context where it is precisely the revolt of goddesses, not (male) gods, that is at issue (103–4; cf. 137–8).

ἀλλὰ μάλ' οὔ πως ἔστι Διὸς νόον αἰγιόχοιο
οὔτε παρεξελθεῖν ἄλλον θεὸν οὔθ' ἁλιῶσαι.

Thus Calypso's rebel, "centrifugal" voice, though it is allowed to surface, is not allowed to stray very far from the center; it is, like her island, lost in the surrounding sea of "centripetal" voices. The voice of the enveloper is itself enveloped.

The second, more daring example of dialogism allows the "centrifugal" voice nearly equivalent status, so much so, in fact, that it came under vigorous censure in antiquity, notably by Xenophanes (fr. 11) and the Platonic Socrates (*Republic* 390c). Even its language displays not a few departures from conventional Homeric forms and usages (see Hainsworth 1986 *ad* 8.266–369). It is the story of Ares, Aphrodite, and Hephaestus sung by Demodocus in book 8. As has often been observed, this tale of the triumph of cunning craft (Hephaestus) over boorish strength (Ares) reiterates the point made in Odysseus's encounter with the handsome but uncivil Euryalus earlier in book 8, and looks ahead to the hero's own account of his victory over the Cyclops in book 9, and ultimately to his conquest of the careless suitors. At first sight, the "centripetal" voice appears to be the stronger, affirming the sanctity of the marriage bond and the sanctions taken against adulterers. An assembly of the gods gathers to determine the fate of the trapped adulterers; the goddesses, in the conventional modesty expected of them, remain at home (8.323).[14] A

---

[14] Like their divine counterparts in the tale, there are no Phaeacian

sober and unsmiling Poseidon promises to give Hephaestus satisfaction, should Ares fail to pay his fine. A terse apothegm of conventional wisdom serves as moral to the tale (329):

οὐκ ἀρετᾷ κακὰ ἔργα· κιχάνει τοι βραδὺς ὠκύν.

(Crime wins no prizes; the gimp outruns the sprinter.)

A purely conventional, moral fable would have ended there. But Demodocus's story gives an uninhibited, uncensored, and unanswered voice to unlawful sexual desire of the very kind Ares is punished for. So startlingly uninhibited is this "centrifugal" voice, especially following as hard as it does on the heels of the moral just mentioned, that this particular passage became a special target for censorship, in a tale already considered unfit, at least as early as the Alexandrians (see Hainsworth 1986: 277; Bolling 1925: 237). Apollo asks Hermes if he would want to lie with Aphrodite thus tightly constrained by bonds. The Border-crosser answers (338–42):

αἲ γὰρ τοῦτο γένοιτο, ἄναξ ἑκατηβόλ᾽ Ἄπολλον·
δεσμοὶ μὲν τρὶς τόσσοι ἀπείρονες ἀμφὶς ἔχοιεν,
ὑμεῖς δ᾽ εἰσορόῳτε θεοὶ πᾶσαί τε θέαιναι,
αὐτὰρ ἐγὼν εὕδοιμι παρὰ χρυσέῃ Ἀφροδίτῃ.

(Exactly what I wish for, Lord Apollo, Shooter from afar! The bonds wrapped round me could be three times as strong, infinite in length, and this in full view of all you gods, and all the goddesses as well; no matter, I'd still want to sleep beside golden Aphrodite.)

Twice the story puts the gods into a fit of laughter: once at the stratagem that traps the adulterous lovers, the second time at this remark of Hermes, as if to endorse each voice. And the whole tale ends with the vision of Aphrodite the laughter-loving (the only occurrence of φιλομμειδής in

women on hand to hear Demodocus's story. Its bawdy content suggests that it was designed for social contexts that exclude women.

the *Odyssey*) on Paphos, still remote from her husband and untouched by punishment, freshly bathed, "a marvelous thing to look at" (θαῦμα ἴδεσθαι, 366).

These are but two among a number of shorter narrative segments where opposing ideological voices can be heard. But what about the bias of the *Odyssey*'s whole narrative frame? How, in other words, does it end? For the case of the *Thousand and One Nights* teaches us that the manner in which a larger narrative frame finds closure may qualitatively surpass in power a host of contrary voices raised within it. Our investigation carries us to that topic in the next chapter.

Chapter 3

POLYTLAS: THE ENDS OF THE *ODYSSEY*

> The way Homer's epics begin in the middle and do
> not finish at the end is a reflection of the truly epic
> mentality's total indifference to any form of
> architectural construction.
> —Georg Lukács, *Theory of the Novel*

> Truth is the predicate at last discovered, the subject
> at last provided with its complement; since the
> character, if we grasped it merely on the level of the
> story's *development*, i.e., from an epic viewpoint,
> would always appear incomplete, unsaturated, a
> subject wandering in search of its final predicate. . . .
> Disclosure is then the final stroke by which the initial
> "probable" shifts to the "necessary."
> —Roland Barthes, *S/Z*

> Nothing in lived reality is closed.
> —Paul Zumthor, *Speaking of the Middle Ages*

IN THE LAST chapter, we discussed a universal formal model of narrative articulated by Claude Bremond. We ended by speaking of contending ideological "voices" that utilize, as it were, the two possible variants on that model. Even on this purely formal level, the *Odyssey*'s attempt to combine the two opposing strategies of myth and *Märchen*, without, as in the *Thousand and One Nights*, subduing one to the other or collapsing one into mere formulaic epilogue for the other, creates a real problem: how is this composite, hybrid narrative to conclude, without doing too much violence to one or the other of its contending voices? This problem—"How is the tale to end?"—this self-conscious narrative, at its very outset, actually absorbs into its own substance, presenting it explicitly as a pair of conflicting views about divine justice. At 1.31ff., Zeus propounds the thesis that, if men suffer *hyper moron*—that is, beyond their natural share of god-sent evils, it is because of moral wrong, *atasthaliai*; he cites the concrete example of Aegisthus. Athena counters with the case of Odysseus, so long kept away from his home, unjustly, if Zeus's thesis is sound. Zeus answers that Poseidon is the cause, unrelenting in his anger for the blinding of his son Polyphemus. And the process of bringing Odysseus home is only initiated in the conveniently motivated absence of Poseidon from Olympus.

In the closing books of the *Odyssey*, there are so many *proximate* narrative ends achieved that we may not be unsatisfied by the lack of clarity surrounding the outcome of the *ultimate end*. Father has come home to son, husband has been reunited with wife, son reunited with aging father, the threat of the suitors erased, and even the countervengeance of the suitors' relatives easily—perhaps too easily—arbitrated by Athena *ex machina*.

What is this *telos* I am calling "ultimate"—the one whose deferred outcome tends to be assumed or simply forgotten in the face of the chain reaction of climaxes with which the poem concludes? We are prepared for it in book 11 with Odysseus's visit to the Underworld to consult the prophet Tiresias. Not the least of problems in this passage is the open tension between function and motivation, so undisguised that it has led to serious charges of interpolation—by one critic, of everything from 10.489 to 12.38.[1] The visit to Tiresias is motivated as follows: beginning at

---

[1] The *Nekyia* is, as so many have insisted, superficially unnecessary to the plot. See Page 1955: 21–51. Wilamowitz (1884: 144) claims that such problems of the plot can be resolved by removing everything between 10.489 and 12.38. Theiler (1950: 105) suggests the removal of everything between 10.489 and 12.23, even though there remains, as he himself observed, a discomfiting difficulty: the conversation in book 10 takes place by night, and the one in book 12 by day.

10.490, Circe tells Odysseus he must go to the realm of the dead to learn from the blind prophet ὁδὸν καὶ μέτρα κελεύθου νόστον θ' (10.539–40)—the measured or measurable stages of his journey home. But Tiresias tells him nothing about the ὁδὸς καὶ μέτρα κελεύθου, and precious little about the νόστος or homecoming, but concentrates on the aftermath of the return and the propitiation of Poseidon. Odysseus then returns to Circe's island for the obsequies of Elpenor, whose accidental death at the end of book 10 had gone unnoticed but whose shade was the first one encountered by Odysseus in book 11. After the funeral rites, Circe herself tells Odysseus the ὁδὸς καὶ μέτρα κελεύθου—the measured stages represented by the Sirens, the Wandering Rocks, Scylla and Charybdis, and the Cattle of the Sun, ending where Tiresias had begun (compare 12.137–41 with 11.110–14).

Clearly, the function of Elpenor's death is to return Odysseus to Circe in order to get a forecast of the adventures in book 12. The motivation seems a flimsy, patched affair: Elpenor's death is accidental and unnoticed; an extrinsic, untragic moral standard of verisimilitude appears to be at work, requiring that his character be just contemptible enough in some measure to deserve or justify his death. He was the youngest of Odysseus's men, we are told, and not a terribly good warrior, nor were his wits very well put together. Few critics have been more explicit (or more exaggerated) about the moralizing dimension in this passage than Alexander Pope, who calls Elpenor's death a "punishment" in a note to his translation:

> Homer dismisses not the description of this house of Pleasure and Debauch, without shewing the Moral of his Fable which is the ill consequences that attend those who indulge themselves in sensuality; this is set forth in the punishment of Elpenor. He describes him as a person of no worth, to shew that debauchery ennervates our faculties, and renders both the mind and body incapable of thinking, or acting with greatness and bravery. At the same time these circumstantial

relations are not without a good effect; for they render the story probable, as if it were spoken with veracity of an History, not the liberty of Poetry.

Something quite incontestable emerges from all this. It is the fact that the motivation cited in book 10 for the visit to Tiresias in book 11 is definitely not its function, for Circe fulfills that function herself in book 12. This has the effect of drawing our attention all the more, as literary sleuths if not as beguiled readers, to the question of function in the visit to Tiresias.

Note, furthermore, that this visit to Tiresias, even on the surface of the narrative, is represented as a necessity. In fact, it is the only segment of Odysseus's passage between Troy and Ithaca that is imposed as a requirement (see Segal 1962: 40): ἀλλ᾽ ἄλλην χρὴ πρῶτον ὁδὸν τελέσαι (10.490). Yet this overcompensation on the surface level of motivation all but disguises the function as well as the flimsiness of the rationale for the journey. Here and elsewhere it would appear that insistence on necessity at the surface or motivational level is inversely proportional to arbitrariness of function. What we have here is something closely akin to the linguistic and mythic processes described by Barthes[2] whereby what is merely arbitrary is made to seem necessary or natural.

But there is something else unusual about this passage—this one, and another closely associated with it in function, the ultimate fate of the Phaeacians at the hands of Poseidon in book 13. In both cases two pertinent questions pose themselves: Why does the poet eschew the otherwise inviolable penchant of oral poetry to fulfill its forecasts and expectancies? Why does he also avoid the often fortuitously "happy" ending of *Märchen*? The question can be posed in somewhat different terms: why do these two epi-

[2] Barthes 1983: 285, quoted above, p. 29. See also his "Myth Today" (1972: 109–59). Compare Hoelscher's comment: "What in the logic of the simple story is miraculous coincidence, is divine dispensation on the level of the epic" (1978: 58).

sodes resist the introduction of casual or accidental circumstances and stop short of resolution?[3] What I shall try
to show is that the demands of the mythic narrative ideology, the "centripetal" voice that tends toward the tragic,
characterized by what Aristotle calls necessity or high
probability and the strongest component of which is the
unappeasable power of Poseidon, neutralize the thrust of
the *Märchen*, the "centrifugal" voice, whose progression is
sustained more by human desire than by "necessity." A
Lévi-Straussian way of reading these two instances of narrative aporia would be to see them as examples of break-
down in an attempt to bridge the discomfitting disconti-
nuity between *nature* (exemplified by the demands of
Poseidon on Zeus) and *culture* (exemplified by the demands of Athena on Zeus), each represented specifically
as a different kind of justice. A Bakhtinian reading would
see the resultant narrative as a dialogic text, in which neither of the contending voices is allowed to dominate.

Let us turn our attention to that prophecy now. Tiresias
speaks of an inland journey to be undertaken by Odysseus,
a journey to a saltless people, ignorant of sea, ship, and
oar. This haunting statement, repeated nearly verbatim by
the hero to Penelope in book 23, quickens the imagination,
lending it a momentum that carries it beyond the text itself
for an answer to the question "What finally happens to
Odysseus?"

νόστον δίζηαι μελιηδέα, φαίδιμ' 'Οδυσσεῦ·   100
τόν δέ τοι ἀργαλέον θήσει θεός. οὐ γὰρ ὀίω
λήσειν ἐννοσίγαιον, ὅ τοι κότον ἔνθετο θυμῷ,
χωόμενος ὅτι οἱ υἱὸν φίλον ἐξαλάωσας.
ἀλλ' ἔτι μέν κε καὶ ὧς, κακά περ πάσχοντες, ἵκοισθε,
αἴ κ' ἐθέλῃς σὸν θυμὸν ἐρυκακέειν καὶ ἑταίρων,   105
ὁππότε κεν πρῶτον πελάσῃς εὐεργέα νῆα
Θρινακίῃ νήσῳ, προφυγὼν ἰοειδέα πόντον,
βοσκομένας δ' εὕρητε βόας καὶ ἴφια μῆλα

---

[3] Among the many problems associated with the *Nekyia*, this strangely
appears to be one that did not interest Page.

Ἠελίου, ὃς πάντ' ἐφορᾷ καὶ πάντ' ἐπακούει.
τὰς εἰ μέν κ' ἀσινέας ἐάᾳς νόστου τε μέδηαι,   110
καί κεν ἔτ' εἰς Ἰθάκην, κακά περ πάσχοντες, ἵκοισθε·
εἰ δέ κε σίνηαι, τότε τοι τεκμαίρομ' ὄλεθρον
νηί τε καὶ ἑτάροισ'. αὐτὸς δ' εἴ πέρ κεν ἀλύξῃς,
ὀψὲ κακῶς νεῖαι, ὀλέσας ἄπο πάντας ἑταίρους,
νηὸς ἐπ' ἀλλοτρίης· δήεις δ' ἐν πήματα οἴκῳ,   115
ἄνδρας ὑπερφιάλους, οἵ τοι βίοτον κατέδουσι
μνώμενοι ἀντιθέην ἄλοχον καὶ ἕδνα διδόντες.
ἀλλ' ἦ τοι κείνων γε βίας ἀποτείσεαι ἐλθών·
αὐτὰρ ἐπὴν μνηστῆρας ἐνὶ μεγάροισι τεοῖσι
κτείνῃς ἠὲ δόλῳ ἢ ἀμφαδὸν ὀξέι χαλκῷ   120
ἔρχεσθαι δὴ ἔπειτα, λαβὼν εὐῆρες ἐρετμόν,
εἰς ὅ κε τοὺς ἀφίκηαι, οἳ οὐκ ἴσασι θάλασσαν
ἀνέρες οὐδέ θ' ἅλεσσι μεμιγμένον εἶδαρ ἔδουσιν·
οὐδ' ἄρα τοὶ ἴσασι νέας φοινικοπαρήους,
οὐδ' εὐήρε' ἐρετμά, τά τε πτερὰ νηυσὶ πέλονται.   125
σῆμα δέ τοι ἐρέω μάλ' ἀριφραδές, οὐδέ σε λήσει·
ὁππότε κεν δή τοι συμβλήμενος ἄλλος ὁδίτης
φήῃ ἀθηρηλοιγὸν ἔχειν ἀνὰ φαιδίμῳ ὤμῳ,
καὶ τότε δὴ γαίῃ πήξας εὐῆρες ἐρετμόν,
ἔρξας ἱερὰ καλὰ Ποσειδάωνι ἄνακτι,   130
ἀρνειὸν ταῦρόν τε συῶν τ' ἐπιβήτορα κάπρον,
οἴκαδ' ἀποστείχειν ἔρδειν θ' ἱεράς ἑκατόμβας
ἀθανάτοισι θεοῖσι, τοὶ οὐρανὸν εὐρὺν ἔχουσι,
πᾶσι μάλ' ἑξείης. θάνατος δέ τοι ἐξ ἁλὸς αὐτῷ
ἀβληχρὸς μάλα τοῖος ἐλεύσεται, ὅς κέ σε πέφνῃ   135
γήρᾳ ὕπο λιπαρῷ ἀρημένον· ἀμφὶ δὲ λαοὶ
ὄλβιοι ἔσσονται. τὰ δέ τοι νημερτέα εἴρω.

([100] Your goal, glorious Odysseus, is a homecoming sweet as honey. Bitter it will be; the god will see to that. There's no evading the Earthshaker, I think, whose rancor at you runs deep for the blinding of his son. Even so, despite harsh suffering, you may make it home, [105] if you resolve to curb your own desire and your men's when first you make land at the island Thrinacia, a fugitive from the purple sea, and find there the cattle and rich flocks of Helios, who sees and hears all. [110] If you leave them unharmed, mind fixed on home-coming, you may all yet come to Ithaca, despite harsh suffering. But if you harm them, you can surely count on doom for ship and crew; even supposing you survive, a late home-coming and a hard one it will be, [115] under an alien sail, all your shipmates lost to you. At home more cause for pain waits: insolent men eating away your life's work, courting your godlike wife with rich gifts. If you make it home, you will no doubt pay back their violence in kind. [119] But when through stealth or open fight your bronze edge brings them down in the halls, then, bearing a balanced oar, set out again until you reach a people ignorant of sea and salted food and ships with bows of crimson, [125] and balanced oars, the wings on which they fly. And this will be a sign, inescapably clear, to know the place: when someone meets you on the road and takes for a winnowing-fan your shouldered oar, calling it "chaff-ravager," then fix in the earth your balanced oar, [130] make fit offerings to Lord Poseidon—ram, bull, and buck boar, mounter of sows—and on return home, holy hecatombs in due order to all wide heaven's deathless gods. Your death will come to you out of the sea, [135] ever so gently, to finish you weary with unwrinkled age, a prosperous people around you. These words are unerring.)

We may well ask what function is served by this impulse to stretch out the plot beyond the formal limits of the text, for within it we learn nothing more of the journey or its outcome. From a narratological point of view this is especially strange, in that the forecast can be seen as belonging to a limited class of narrative whose hallmark is the difficult or impossible prophecy fulfilled, or the seemingly impossible task performed. Its essence absolutely requires the explicit narration—never the mere presumption—of fulfillment, for the fulfillment stands as solution to the puzzle posed in the prophecy (or task imposed). The plot of the killing of the suitors is another instance, posing as it does a seemingly impossible situation: one man against 108. Other examples are the tales of Alcmaeon and Mac-

beth, the one cursed never to escape the Erinyes until he
finds a land that did not exist when he killed his mother
(Thuc. 2.102.5–6), and the other promised never to be
vanquished "until / Great Birnam wood to high Dunsinane
hill / Shall come against him" (Shakespeare, *Macbeth*
4.1.92–94). Such a narrative proposition without an explicit rendering of its outcome is surely unusual if not in-
tolerable. Furthermore, the unusual expression used for a
winnowing-fan at 11.128, *athērēloigos* ("chaff-ravager"),
suggests a kind of folktale spell-breaking formula that anticipates its own enactment, but never merely silently presumes it.[4]

In itself this would make it difficult to assume, as it has
been too easily assumed, that the poet meant the fulfillment of Tiresias's prophecy about Odysseus's gentle death
to be an unqualified certitude. But such an assumption
further disregards certain logical and linguistic peculiari-
ties of the passage in question. Philological speculation on
these lines suffered an unfortunate derailment when it
converged on line 134 for major comment: *ex halos*—does
it mean "out of the sea," "away from the sea," or "just dis-
embarked"? To be sure, the *ex halos* problem is important,
another rich ambiguity that perhaps pleases the imagination by puzzling it, but it should not distract attention from
a prior and at once more fundamental and significant feature of the prophecy: its conditional nature.[5] In this as in

---

[4] Dornseiff (1937: 353), for example, speaking of the words to be used
by that inland traveller in mistaking the oar for a winnowing-fan as a kind
of folktale spell-breaking formula, says "das erlösende Wort, das gesagt
werden muss, ist so ungewöhnlich, dass die Aussicht, dass bald jemand
gerade dieses Wort sagen wird, erdrückend gering ist, die Reise kann
ausserordenlich lang werden (aber, hoffen wir Leser, Athene wolle ihre
Hilfe auch da nicht versagen)." We shall have considerable cause later to
comment on the unexamined demand for "poetic justice" in his paren-
thetical close.

[5] Page (1955: 49 n. 10) recognizes, as others have, the uncertainty of
lines 100–117, but not of the following portion on the inland journey:
"The peculiar uncertainty of the prophet in this passage has often been

much of Greek prophecy, the seer is less inclined to present a simple and absolute vision of future events than to
illuminate what philosophers would later call certain necessary or probable causal relationships (see Devereux
1968, esp. 452ff). He is less likely to say simply that *B* will
occur, than to say "if *A*, then *B*."[6] What the prophet is represented as knowing is not so much the future as the fact
that there is a measure of order and regularity in events,
that characters and actions issue in definite or usual—and
therefore predictable—outcomes. He does not *see* future
events; he reads their seeds or signs. It is not a matter of
revealing a mystery, but of stating conditioned probabilities.[7] It is not a matter of constricting the field of decision,
but of clarifying the framework within which it operates.[8]
More bluntly: it is the storyteller tipping his hand, showing
us where the story can or will go, because he has already
determined the end.[9]

The prophecy can be conceived as a narrator's grid of
possibilities. Placed at the turning point of the poem it

---

remarked: 105 αἴ κε, 110 εἰ μέν κε, 112 εἰ δέ κε, 113 εἴ πέρ κεν; Tiresias
ought to be able to do better than this."

[6] Cf. Ehnmark 1935: 75: "This conditional prediction is typical. It is
extremely common for an oracle to answer: if you act in such and such a
way, the result will be such and such. . . . The oracle foretells the future
subject to certain conditions; it can predict the consequences of a certain
course of action. Such prophecies presuppose the existence of an order,
or regularity in what happens, which yet leaves some scope for the free
decisions of the individual. This order is something altogether abstract,
being neither power, nor will, nor person. It is a scheme of events, not a
power that controls them." I would argue against Ehnmark's otherwise
excellent summation that this so-called "scheme of events" is a complex
dialogic adjustment between traditional and conventional norms of verisimilitude and the poet's sense of his own power over his narrative materials.

[7] Tiresias's τεκμαίρομ(αι) (112) has the ring of a Thucydidean inference.

[8] Failure to see this leads Page to say, as we observed in note 5 above,
"Tiresias ought to be able to do better than this." But on his assumption,
he could have gone yet further: Tiresias does not even see clearly how
Odysseus is to kill the suitors—ἠὲ δόλῳ ἢ ἀμφαδόν (120).

[9] Compare the quotation from Valery, p. 42 above.

both summarizes the turns of plot that have kept the story going so far, and anticipates the possibilities in the tale's future. It is both review and preview from the still, timeless perspective of death, almost outside the plot, as it were.[10] The prophecy proceeds, like Bremond's model, through a series of consecutive pairs of alternatives, each pair (after the first) dependent upon only *one* of the two previous alternatives, while the other is discarded. Thus:

> Given *A* or *B*;
> if *B*, then *C* or *D*;
> if *D*, then *E* or *F*, and so forth.

Figure 3 shows the prophecy schematized à la Bremond. Paraphrasing the prophecy so as to make more explicit the conditional nature of the clauses:

> You will either make land at Thrinacia or not; if you do, you will either injure the cattle of Helios or not; if you do, either all of you will perish, or you alone[11] will escape; if you escape, get home, and gain vengeance, etc., you will undertake a search that will either be successful or unsuccessful; if suc-

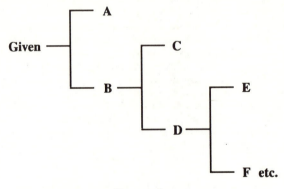

FIGURE 3.

[10] See note 1 above.
[11] See Denniston 1934: 488 n. 1 on εἴ πέρ. See also Page 1955: 27–28: "Even his own [sc. Odysseus's] escape is left in doubt."

cessful, you will return home and eventually die a gentle death.

Parenthetically, the form of my paraphrase is in fact used by another prophet, Proteus, in *Odyssey* 4 when, in reference to Aegisthus, he tells Menelaus (546–47):

ἢ γάρ μιν ζωόν γε κιχήσεαι, ἢ κεν Ὀρέστης
κτεῖνεν ὑποφθάμενος· σὺ δέ κεν τάφου ἀντιβολήσαις.

(Either you'll return to find him [Aegisthus] alive, or Orestes has killed him before you; [if the latter,] then you'll come home to a funeral.)

In Tiresias's prophecy, then, the final result—the conclusion of the story in effect—is tied to four consecutive conditions without any prediction as to their fulfillment. Now, of course, from the first twenty lines of the poem, from Zeus's assurance that Odysseus will in fact reach home (1.76–79), and more obviously from the fact that it is Odysseus himself who is relating these events sometime after the accomplishment of most of them, the audience has no trouble inferring the fulfillment of all but the last condition. In short, while Tiresias may be in doubt about the fulfillment of the conditions of his prophecy, the audience from the very beginning, and at many stages throughout the poem, is made privy to the narrator's assurance of the hero's survival, homecoming, and revenge. But the outcome of the inland journey—the last condition—is another matter. Here the reader loses his advantage over Tiresias, and must share his blindness and his uncertainty.

Schematically, the narrative potentialities in the prophecy may be represented as shown in Figure 4. An immediate objection to this way of looking at the passage might be to say that the inland journey is, in fact, no real condition; that when Tiresias says "Go inland until you find a people that does not know the sea, etc.," there is never any real doubt about the outcome; that just as Tiresias always moves from one pair of alternatives to the next by choos-

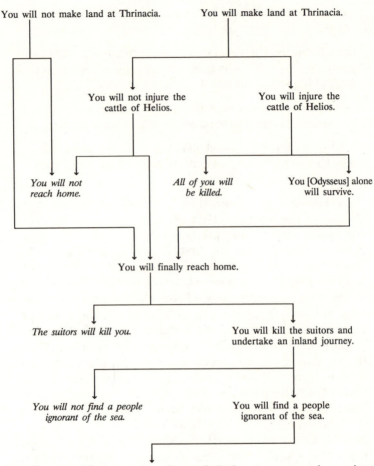

FIGURE 4.
Italics indicate eventualities on which, if actualized, the narrative
would conclude.

ing the condition that will in fact prevail, so here when he makes the success of the inland search a condition of Odysseus's final return and gentle death, we must assume without question the success of the search. It should be understood first that whatever view one may be inclined to hold in this matter, the syntax of the prophecy is of no particular help. When they are cast in the present tense, *until* clauses, in Greek as in English, are of two distinct types.[12] One implies an eventuality certain to be achieved, as in the following example (*Il.* 14.77–78):

ὕψι δ᾽ ἐπ᾽ εὐνάων ὁρμίσσομεν εἰς ὅ κεν ἔλθῃ
νὺξ ἀβρότη.

(Let us moor [the ships] at anchor stones in deep water, until immortal Night comes.)

The other type implies an eventuality not certain to be achieved, as in these two examples (*Il.* 3.290, *Od.* 22.72–73):

μαχήσομαι . . . ἥός τε τέλος πολέμοιο κιχείω.

(I shall fight until I reach an end of my quarrel.)

τοξάσσεται εἰς ὅ κε πάντας
ἄμμε κατακτείνῃ.

(He will shoot the bow until he kills us all.)

In the first case, the meaning is "until X occurs" with virtually absolute predictability as to its eventual occurrence; in the second case, there is less assurance as to its eventual occurrence, or at least what might be called the "zero-grade" of certainty. When placed in the past tense, the distinction is evident in the syntax. The speaker can, with respect to a past action, express either the moment of uncertainty prior to occurrence (e.g., in *Od.* 12.437–38, the first example below) or a perspective that leaves no doubt about

---

[12] Note that the prophecies in the stories of Alcmaeon and Macbeth referred to above also employ *until* clauses.

occurrence (e.g., in *Od.* 7.280–81, the second example below):

νωλεμέως δ᾽ ἐχόμην, ὄφρ᾽ ἐξεμέσειεν ὀπίσσω
ἱστὸν καὶ τρόπιν αὖτις. ἐελδομένῳ δέ μοι ἦλθον.

(I clung relentlessly [to the fig tree] until [Charybdis] *should* spout back again my mast and keel [= . . . to see if Charybdis *would* spout back, etc.]. In the midst of my hope they came back to me.)

νῆχον πάλιν εἷος ἐπῆλθον
εἰς ποταμόν.

(I swam back until I reached the river.)

Unfortunately for our problem, the syntactic construction of both types in the present tense is the same. In practice, content and context are usually sufficient to distinguish one type from the other, for a framework of verisimilitude normally operates to separate sure eventualities from unsure ones. Not so in the present passage. I say that content and context are *usually* sufficient, unless, of course, the semantic situation is complicated by deception (always a possibility), as when Penelope asks the suitors not to press the marriage *until* she finishes weaving (literally, brings to a *telos*) Laertes' burial shroud (2.97–98):

μίμνετ᾽ ἐπειγόμενοι τὸν ἐμὸν γάμον, εἰς ὅ κε φᾶρος
ἐκτελέσω.

(Hold back in urging marriage on me, until I complete [Laertes'] shroud.)

As it stands, the statement belongs to our first type; it appears to have a predictable outcome. Indeed, its success as deception depends upon such an expectancy. But Penelope's true state of mind belongs to our second type; it implies an outcome uncertain to her: what she *intends* is to delay marriage *until* either Odysseus returns or she receives unimpeachable proof of his death, neither of which events seems assured. What the suitors take as a predictable conclusion is a disguise for what she sees as an unpredictable condition. But more later of Penelope's evasive tactics and their relation to the poet's. The main point here is that, if we are to infer that Odysseus would eventually find the strange people mentioned by Tiresias, it cannot be on the basis of the syntax, content, or immediate context of this passage. In fact, the surest guide we possess upon which to base our own response to the prophecy is the response of Penelope when she hears it (23.286–87), and that, as we shall see, simply reinforces the ambivalence of the prophecy with its own ambivalence and guarded conditionality.

From the fact that the inland journey is the only condition in Tiresias's prophecy that is not fulfilled within the poem, are we to assume that this passage was referring to a story so well known by its audience that it needed no explicit conclusion? A commonplace of the narrative tradition that localized the completion of Odysseus's inland journey at some more or less definite point, whether geographically identifiable or merely fabulous? Or are we to assume that this passage is perhaps more in the nature of a transition piece to some other narrative than an integral and organic component of the *Odyssey*? Did Eugammon's *Telegony* rely on such a current story, or did he take up the uncertain cue offered by the *Odyssey* and freely invent, as would a host of others after him? We cannot find certain answers to these questions. In the *Telegony*, according to Proclus's summary in the *Chrestomathy*, Odysseus visits Elis, where he is entertained by King Polyxenus, and then returns to Ithaca to perform the sacrifices enjoined by Tiresias. Leaving Ithaca again, he reaches the country of the Thesprotians, marries their queen Callidice,[13] commands

---

[13] An unusual, bigamous marriage which, right from the start, should give us pause in assuming close and consistent ties between the *Telegony* and the *Odyssey*. It is at least as reasonable, perhaps more so, to assume

their forces in a war against the Brygians, and many years later, after the death of the queen, returns to Ithaca, leaving Polypoetes, his son by Callidice, to rule the Thesprotians. Back in Ithaca, Telegonus, Odysseus's son by Circe, comes in search of his father, kills him unwittingly with a spear barbed with a sting-ray spine, and conveys his body, together with Penelope and Telemachus, back to Circe. Through her charms the three mortals become immortal, and, as if the barrier of the burlesque had yet to be breached, Telegonus marries Penelope, and Telemachus Circe, and they all quite literally live happily ever after!

That is a good example of what I mean by the *Märchen* perspective,[14] but our present concern is with the treatment of the inland journey and its aftermath by Eugammon and others. It would take much time to focus on such post-Homeric attempts to conclude the *Odyssey*, but if we did we should only find that we had come up a blind alley. (For a recent account of this matter, see Hansen 1977.) If I may summarize, we would find that these accounts not only contradict one another, but—a more serious defect— none of them quite fulfills the precise terms of Tiresias's prophecy. The major contender for the honor of "completing" the *Odyssey*—the *Telegony*—suggests anything but the gentle death spoken of by Tiresias, and this has prompted a curious rationalization by one critic: "es ist für einem alten Menschen kein leidloserer Tod denkbar also plötzlich einen Stich ins Herz zu bekommen" (Dornseiff 1937: 354). In the final analysis, I would submit, we are forced to view the *Odyssey* as it lies before us, disengaged from an author-subject or author-subjects, leaving aside the consideration of presumed pre-Homeric or mythic models, and resisting the temptation to ferret out hypothetical post-Homeric *bearbeiter* and interpolators, whose

---

that the *Telegony* was based less closely on the *Odyssey* than on the *Thesprotis*, in which Penelope was dismissed for adultery.

[14] This situation prompted Eustathius (1796.35) to comment περιττὰ ταῦτα καὶ κενὴ μοχθηρία!

"unauthentic" additions are assumed to have contradicted or disguised the meaning of some hypothetical *echt Odyssey*.

. . .

We started by proposing that the outcome of the inland journey is a more or less deliberate ambiguity, like Penelope's delaying tactic—deliberate in the sense of *functional*. As preliminary justification for this point of view we observed that of all the conditions mentioned by Tiresias it is the only one that the reader or listener does not see fulfilled. It remains to analyze the functional role of this ambiguity. But we may be in a somewhat better position to do this after considering what freedom the poet (or poem) may have had to certify the outcome of the prophecy, had he (or it) so intended. It is not beside the point to ask whether means were at hand of enclosing the important element of Poseidon's appeasement *within* the *Odyssey*, thus giving the work the closed, architectural, more finished form one associates with the *Iliad*.[15] In other words, if the necessity to placate the god is absolute (and that I take to be axiomatic),[16] would this element not have been more neatly incorporated into the tale by fulfilling Odysseus's inland journey before his return to Ithaca and vengeance on the suitors—again, assuming the poet had so wished it? This is not so fanciful as it may at first sight appear, for the conditions of such an arrangement are in fact advanced right within the *Odyssey* itself, as if the text were, from a

[15] On some special problems of closure in the *Iliad*, minor by comparison with the one that we are here dealing with, see Redfield 1975: 204–23. On general problems of literary closure, see Smith 1968.

[16] As against Woodhouse (1930: 39), who claims that the wrath of Poseidon "is merely a temporary motive of convenience, to be silently dropped, just as was that of Athena, and that of Helios also, when it had served its turn." One objection, at least, to this simplification is that the wraths of Athena and Helios are indeed dropped, but only after the offending parties have been destroyed. In the system of verisimilitude that controls the Homeric poems, wrath appears to be a social and political response, not a passing tantrum. It requires compensation.

Bremondian perspective, openly previewing its own potential conclusions.

In the lie that disguised Odysseus tells Eumaeus (14.314–33) and, with greater detail, Penelope (19.269–307), he reconstructs the course of his adventures as follows: from Thrinacia, where he loses ship and crew, he is washed ashore on the island of the Phaeacians, who in the end escort him with many gifts *not home to Ithaca but to Thesprotia*. (Remember that in Eugammon's *Telegony*, it is on his return from Thesprotia that Odysseus is killed by Telegonus.) For an indeterminate period of time he knocks about amassing a fortune, leaving it in the custody of the Thesprotian king Pheidon, who has promised him ship and crew for the return home. At the point when the lie is told, Odysseus is alleged to be consulting the oracle at Dodona whether to return home "openly or secretly" (ἢ ἀμφαδὸν ἦε κρυφηδόν, 14.330 = 19.299: shades of Tiresias's ἠὲ δόλῳ ἢ ἀμφαδόν, 11.120). Here in brief outline is the structure of an *Odyssey* that would have permitted the hero to complete his inland journey in central Epirus within the confines of the work itself, a structure, furthermore, to which, curiously enough, the invocation in *Od.* 1.1–10 is far more appropriate than to the actual *Odyssey*.[17]

Our hypothetical work would have ended with the powers of nature fully placated and the local social order of Ithaca, though severely dislocated by the extent of the hero's vengeance, finally subject to the absolute guarantee of

---

[17] πολλῶν δ'ἀνθρώπων ἴδεν ἄστεα ("He saw the towns of many people," 1.3) fits the action of the lie in book 19 far better than that of the actual *Odyssey*, and in book 23, just before Odysseus recounts Tiresias's prophecy to Penelope, he tells her that the prophet has bid him travel to many towns of men (μάλα πολλὰ βροτῶν ἐπὶ ἄστε' ἀνωγεν / ἐλθεῖν, 267). Compare also statements in the lies: αὐτὰρ ἐγώγε / πολλὰ βροτῶν ἐπὶ ἄστε' ἀλώμενος ἐνθάδ' ἱκάνω (15.491); πολλὰ βροτῶν ἐπὶ ἄστε' ἀλώμενος, ἄλγεα πάσχων (19.170). About the blinding of Polyphemus and the anger of Poseidon, both the invocation and the lie are silent. And the Helios episode, with which the invocation is preoccupied, rather out of proportion to its importance in the poem, is precisely the episode with which the lie begins.

restoration. The poem would thus have projected the image of a universe, like the one we find in *Märchen*, full of hostility to be sure, but, so far as Odysseus is concerned, not ultimately "unjust."

Another characteristic of this hypothetical structure is that it would maintain what we have already noted as a rarely violated penchant of oral poetry to fulfill its forecasts and expectancies. It would be difficult to cite a more characteristic structural feature of Homeric as of all epic poetry than the process of advancing one's narrative by this method of foreshadow and fulfillment, ranging from the obscure form of dream and omen, through the twilight zone of not-unimpeachable human seers, to the unmistakable prophecy of a god and the explicit forecast of the narrator. It is largely this characteristic which endows the Homeric moral universe with what many readers have read as a sense of regularity, of law, of that necessity or high probability which Aristotle admired in tragic plots, and which Bakhtin would doubtless attribute to the "centripetal" voice. Yet there are two instances in the Homeric poems of unfulfilled expectancy, instances that cannot be attributed to forgetfulness, for they are both emotionally charged matters, critical to the development of the plot, and further underscored with emphasis by repetition. One of them is the inland journey. The other is so intimately involved with it, so identical in function, that they may be treated as doublets that illuminate one another. This second unfulfilled expectancy is the ultimate fate of the Phaeacians at the hands of Poseidon.

At the end of book 8, in Alcinous's account of his father Nausithous's prophecy, we learn that Poseidon had conceived (or would conceive) a grudge against the Phaeacians for escorting men over the high seas without hazard. One day, the prophecy warns, a returning Phaeacian ship would be wrecked and the city enveloped with a mountain (8.564–71)[18]:

[18] ὄρος πόλει ἀμφικαλύψειν (569). There is some disagreement over

ἀλλὰ τόδ' ὥς ποτε πατρὸς ἐγὼν εἰπόντος ἄκουσα
Ναυσιθόου, ὃς ἔφασκε Ποσειδάων' ἀγάσασθαι   565
ἡμῖν, οὕνεκα πομποὶ ἀπήμονές εἰμεν ἁπάντων·
φῆ ποτε φαιήκων ἀνδρῶν περικαλλέα νῆα
ἐκ πομπῆς ἀνιοῦσαν ἐν ἠεροειδέι πόντῳ
ῥαισέμεναι, μέγα δ' ἥμιν ὄρος πόλει ἀμφικαλύψειν.
ὣς ἀγόρευ' ὁ γέρων· τὰ δέ κεν θεὸς ἢ τελέσειεν,   570
ἤ κ' ἀτέλεστ' εἴη, ὥς οἱ φίλον ἔπλετο θυμῷ.

(There is something I once heard my father Nausithous say: that Poseidon had conceived a grudge against us for escorting people over the high seas without hazard. He said that some day he would wreck one of our lovely ships homeward bound from escort on the misty sea, and overwhelm our city with a huge mountain. Those were the old man's words. These things the god may bring to fulfillment or leave unfulfilled, as suits his pleasure.)

Later, in book 13, after the Phaeacians have escorted Odysseus to Ithaca, Poseidon complains to Zeus of his severely diminished honor (*timē*). Zeus reassures him that his *timē* is not and never will be in jeopardy, and in unusually deferential terms bids him do what he pleases in the matter (145): ἔρξον ὅπως ἐθέλεις καί τοι φίλον ἔπλετο θυμῷ. Poseidon's pleasure is precisely to fulfill the terms of Nausithous's prophecy. Zeus agrees and even suggests, as a fin-

---

precisely what is meant here. Are the Phaeacians "obliterated" (ἠφανίσθησαν, Aristarchus) or is their city "blotted out" (Bassett 1933)? Is the city "overwhelmed" (*saxis obruta*, van Leeuwen 1917), or hidden *under* a mountain (Bassett 1933)? According to Merry (1887 *ad* 13.152), "Poseidon does not propose to bury the city, but to shut it off from the use of its two harbours by some great mountain mass." This would seem more reasonable by the norms of a verisimilitude that sees divine "justice" in terms of equivalent retaliation. Poseidon's punishment would thus suit the "crime": a ship "as swift as bird or thought" (7.32) is permanently immobilized in stone, and a people with maximal access to the sea is utterly landlocked. This meaning also suits the use of the word at 8.511, where we are told that Troy is fated to perish when the city ἀμφικαλύψῃ ("encloses" or "shuts in" rather than "covers over" or "conceals") the wooden horse.

ishing touch, the ἀπολίθωσις, the petrifaction of the ship. Accordingly, the ship is turned to stone in the sight of the amazed Phaeacians, and Alcinous, again recalling his father's prophecy, initiates sacrifices in the hope that the god might be dissuaded from enveloping the city with a mountain. Without a further word about their ultimate fate, the narrative leaves the Phaeacians standing in prayer around their altar of supplication.

The poem's silence opened the door to critical disagreement at least as early as the Alexandrians themselves. Aristophanes, scandalized by a pusillanimous Zeus who would make himself accessory to the destruction of the Phaeacians, alters μέγα δέ in line 158 to μηδέ, thus changing ". . . overwhelm their city with a *huge* mountain" to ". . . but *don't* overwhelm their city with a mountain." The result is a folktale Zeus as judicious as he is merciful who grants Poseidon his first wish but discourages the second (156–58):

> θεῖναι λίθον ἐγγύθι γαίης
> νηὶ θοῇ ἴκελον ἵνα θαυμάζωσιν ἅπαντες
> ἄνθρωποι, μηδέ σφιν ὄρος πόλει ἀμφικαλύψαι.

(Turn it into a stone that looks like a ship near enough to land that all men may look at it with awe, *but don't* overwhelm their city with a mountain.)

Scholia Z (*ad* 152), Eustathius (1737.20, 26), and apparently all those ancients who took Corcyra for Homer's Scheria agree. So, by the way, do the most popular English translators of the *Odyssey*, Robert Fitzgerald and Richmond Lattimore. But neither Aristarchus (Scholia H *ad* 152, V *ad* 185) nor the Apollodoran *Epitome* (7.25) will have any of that; for them the Phaeacians suffer as predicted. With few exceptions modern critics generally tend to reflect Aristophanes's tender-mindedness. A sample of their comments illustrates how rigorously the demands of an untragic sense of poetic justice have influenced their reading of this passage:

Presumably the Phaeacians are successful in their attempts to avert the catastrophe. (Duckworth 1933: 109n.228)

Homer, master of the narrator's art, is always considerate of the feelings of his audience. The Phaeacians are our friends; they have treated our hero with great kindness and have brought him to Ithaca at last, enriched by their lavish gifts. The destruction of the family of Alcinous, above all, of Nausicaa, for acts of kindness which deserved a reward and gratitude rather than punishment would be σχέτλιον, as Demosthenes says of a lighter punishment in his own case. Therefore the poet's audience must be left with exactly the impression most modern readers have. . . . As we bid them [sc. the Phaeacians] farewell (vss. 185–87) we share their hope of deliverance. No indignation against the poet for treating them so shabbily remains to rankle in our minds. (Bassett 1933: 305–7)

Non perierunt igitur Alcinous, Arete, Laodamus, ceteri qui nobis innotuerunt principes, non periit quam deligere didicimus Nausicaa, non frustra iis optima quaevis modo apprecatus est Ulixes (vs. 44–46, 59–62), neque saxis obruta est urbs spatiosa vel ipsa regia auro resplendens; cuiusmodi quid *neque iustitia poetica ferebat, neque sensus pulcri et decori*. (Van Leeuwen 1917: 364, *ad* 13.153–58)

"Neque iustitia poetica . . . neque sensus pulcri et decori": there is the heart of the matter. For our questions about the inland journey and the fate of the Phaeacians are fundamentally questions of justice—the justice of the tragic myth as against the justice of the *Märchen*.

But besides the fact that the fate of the Phaeacians is not accomplished within the narrative, there are two other extraordinary features of this passage, one of them unparalleled in the Homeric poems, the other paralleled but once, both of them suggesting severe dislocation of traditional narrative technique if not of an inherited tale. One of them is the narrator's failure to report the god's response to a prayer at 13.184ff.[19] The other is more startling still: the change of scene at 187, from Scheria to Ithaca, *in midline* (185–87):

ὣς οἱ μέν ῥ᾽ εὔχοντο Ποσειδάωνι ἄνακτι
δήμου Φαιήκων ἡγήτορες ἠδὲ μέδοντες,
ἑσταότες περὶ βωμόν.
          ὁ δ᾽ ἔγρετο δῖος Ὀδυσσεὺς κτλ.

(Thus the Phaeacian leadership prayed to Lord Poseidon, standing around his altar. But glorious Odysseus awakened. . . .)

Abrupt, large-scale shifts of scene are themselves rare enough, as, for example, *Od.* 4.625, where the narrative moves from Sparta to Ithaca between lines by other than the usual means, but nowhere except at *Iliad* 1.430 (itself problematical) and here at 13.187 does such a shift occur within the line.[20]

It is worth noting that the equivocalness of the narrative here was appreciated by Eustathius despite his belief in the salvation of the Phaeacians (1737.20: ἡ γὰρ τῶν Φαιάκων σώζεται φανερῶς). In his interpretation of this ambiguity, as so often elsewhere in Eustathius, subtlety consorts with silliness to create a fascinating argument: he considers the poet's silence an ingenious and deliberate contrivance to discourage idle curiosity concerning Scheria's whereabouts and to escape a rationalist critique by having it both ways (1737.21: εἰς ἀποφυγὴν ἐλέγχου; cf. 1610.37: οὕτω μένει τὸ ψεῦσμα τοῦ ποιητοῦ ἀνεξέλεγκτον). Such a bizarre picture may be readily dismissed. Not so easily dismissed is the more important basic observation of Eustathius that

[19] Finsler 1918: 2.348. Incidentally, the only extant formula indicating the divine response that would fit the second half of line 187 is negative: ὁ δ᾽ οὐκ ἐμπάζετο ἱρῶν (9.553). No extant formulas indicating a favorable response fit, e.g., τοῦ [τῶν] ἔκλυε κυανοχαίτης.

[20] When I speak of *large-scale* shifts of locale, I do not include those which occur between one part of Ithaca and another at 15.495 and 17.182. These are mid-line shifts and are statistically rare, but they give nothing like the impression of abruptness we get in 13.187 and *Il.* 1.430.

this passage is a remarkable departure from the poet's regular narrative technique.

. . .

What does all this add up to? We are at a major turning point in the poem, where it divides naturally into halves, and where we might have expected a (perhaps final) solution, one way or another, to the plot line fueled by Poseidon's wrath, before taking up the plot chain leading to vengeance against the suitors. Here, where Poseidon confronts Zeus to demand satisfaction, was, we might have thought, a most appropriate point to introduce (or at least to recall) the inland journey of expiation, with perhaps some divine guarantee about its outcome.[21] Instead, Poseidon's anger against Odysseus is effectively repressed or, perhaps better, displaced from the focus of attention by its less critical doublet, the god's anger against the Phaeacians. The structuralist might call this an attempt to overcome a dilemma on one level of the narrative by transferring the terms of the dilemma to another level. But even then, with unparalleled abruptness, we are cut short, with our second dilemma itself unresolved, wondering whether Poseidon is in fact placated by the Phaeacian sacrifice or whether he finally treats them as predicted.

Our general thesis is that many of the narrative idiosyncrasies of the *Odyssey*—idiosyncrasies by the norms of conventional classical philology—can be explained as the collision of, and attempted mediation between, two kinds of narrative ideology: one a "myth" of nature's recalcitrance to culture, of the kind we see perhaps most vividly in the cattle of the sun episode, and the other what Aristotle might have characterized as a philosophically irresponsible *Märchen*, of the kind that surfaces in its purest form in the Menelaus episode of book 4, with its prophecy of Elysion

[21] As, for example, Jupiter's forecast of Rome's greatness in *Aeneid* 1.257–96, which removes from Anchises's prophecy in book 6 the kind of uncertainty we find in Tiresias's speech in *Od.* 11.

and a more or less fortuitously gained immortality for the hero. The large inheritance of *Märchen* in the *Odyssey* has, of course, been long recognized. But my thesis is that the *Märchen* plot development suffers derailment again and again at precisely those points where it would be expected to make an unembarrassed leap into the world of wish-fulfillment or resort to the improbable or accidental, were it free to follow its own dynamics. On the other hand, its obstacle, a tragically oriented myth, is itself hindered by the contradictory claims of the *Märchen* from reaching its expected conclusion. The two passages I have discussed are stratagems of silence to avoid saying "yes" to one system of organizing experience and "no" to another, in a higher and more complicated system, the poem, that only precariously maintains them both. Reflection on the alternatives for concluding the narrative becomes itself an integral component of the narrative, a device in fact for evading conclusion to achieve, however tenuously, a union of its oppositions, a "dialogic" text.

Aristotle's description of the *logos* or "argument" of the *Odyssey* (in *Poetics* 1455b16) is curiously reticent about what I am calling the tragic or "mythic" system, treating it as if the wrath of Poseidon were only a prelude to the presumed substance of the poem, the return of Odysseus and the vengeance on the suitors. It is almost as if he were reluctant to suggest that a narrative of such long-standing prestige as the *Odyssey* has indeed a beginning and a middle, but no end, at least not the kind defined by him. Or else, perhaps more likely, like the suitors, he was duped by the syntactic tactic of a poet who, like Penelope, wanted it both ways.

This analogy between the poet's strategy and Penelope's is not mere whimsy. We have already seen how she uses the same kind of εἰς ὅ κε ("until") clause in book 2 to gain more time. Penelope wants it both ways (1.249–50):

ἡ δ' οὔτ' ἀρνεῖται στυγερὸν γάμον οὔτε τελευτὴν
ποιῆσαι δύναται.

(She neither refused marriage as hateful to her nor is she
able to bring the matter to conclusion.)

When in book 2 Telemachus publicly charges the suitors
with misconduct, Antinous with good cause blames Penelope for having "profiteering guile on her mind" (ἥ τοι
περὶ κέρδεα οἶδεν, 88). For almost four years now, he explains, she has broken the hearts of the suitors, given them
all cause for hope, dispatching promising missives to each.
George Devereux, in a short but cogent piece (1957),
points out what should have been obvious to readers of the
poem all along: that her tears of grief in her dream of
geese slaughtered by an eagle—interpreted right within
the dream itself as the slaughter of the suitors by Odysseus—represent not what psychologists call "inversion of
affect," as Dodds (1957: 106) saw it, but "real affect." "It is
hard to understand," Devereux says (1957: 382),

> how literary critics could have overlooked the obvious fact
> that a rapidly aging woman, denied for some twenty years
> the pleasures of sex and the company and support of a hus-
> band, would inevitably be unconsciously flattered by the at-
> tentions of young and highly eligible suitors, which is pre-
> cisely what the chief suitor accuses her of in public. We
> therefore believe that Penelope cried over her geese for the
> simple reason that unconsciously she enjoyed being courted.

As Penelope herself confesses to disguised Odysseus, her
mind is divided whether to hold out or go off with which-
ever of the suitors proves his superiority by offering her
the biggest brideprice. And her behavior before the suitors
in book 18 is a paradigm of what we might call the lucra-
tive tease. To gain still more time, to maintain yet a little
longer both the dream of Odysseus's return and the pleasure of the suitors' flattery, she uses another semantic ambiguity, closely approximating, if not syntactically identical
to, the *until* clause employed earlier: "I am inclined," she
says, "to go off with whoever most readily strings the bow
and shoots through all twelve axes" (21.75–76):

ὃς δέ κε ῥηίτατ᾽ ἐντανύσῃ βιὸν ἐν παλάμῃσι
καὶ διοϊστεύσῃ πελέκεων δυοκαίδεκα πάντων.

Scholars have long been scandalized by Penelope's action here, most of them considering it a clumsily incorporated episode from an earlier version in which there was full collusion between Odysseus and Penelope in the contest of the bow. Kirk (1962: 246–47) sums up the opinion of those who consider "utterly illogical" Penelope's announcement of the bow contest at this point:

> Evidence has been accumulating all that day that Odysseus is near at hand. . . . Why does she proceed . . . apparently without special reason, to announce a contest which will result in her immediate acceptance of one of her suitors?

But will it? The mistake of Kirk and the other critics is the same as the suitors'. The suitors appear to take her statement as indicative of something sure to be accomplished, that is, *as a way of distinguishing one bridegroom among many suitors*, now that she has, they think, acquiesced to the marriage. But in fact her ὅς κε ("whoever") clause is not only relative but conditional. If in fact, as she may suspect and as it turns out, none of them can perform the task, it can be considered yet another way of gaining more time (see Amory 1960: 116; also Woodhouse 1930: 82–83; Harsh 1950: 13). That and/or a way of testing the suspicion some critics see in her that the beggar may be Odysseus, or, what I find more likely, that the beggar's prophecy about Odysseus's imminent return may be true, coinciding as it does with Theoclymenus's prophecy (17.155–59) and with Halitherses,' pronounced two decades earlier.

. . .

Penelope accomplishes her purpose. Her desire is fulfilled, but only momentarily. For her fate and the outcome of the inland journey are intimately linked. The *Odyssey* does not end with the dream of desire fulfilled, where the folktale would have ended, where both Aristophanes and Aristarchus—at this point at least, bad critics but good lovers—would have it end, in the nuptial embrace of Odysseus and Penelope (23.296).[22] That moment is marred by the shadow of the future, Tiresias's prophecy. Compelled by Penelope before love-making to tell the tale, Odysseus answers, "Your heart will take no joy in it, nor I in telling it" (266–67):

οὐ μέν τοι θυμὸς κεχαρήσεται· οὐδὲ γὰρ αὐτὸς
χαίρω.

Deprived of suitors, deprived again of a husband, Penelope utters her last words in the poem, words in which it is hard not to find some disappointment, if not bitterness—words, in any case, whose interpretation will be a microcosmic icon of how one reads the entire poem (286):

εἰ μὲν δὴ γῆράς γε θεοὶ τελέουσιν ἄρειον
ἐλπωρή τοι ἔπειτα κακῶν ὑπάλυξιν ἔσεσθαι.

(If indeed the gods are going to bring to fulfillment an old age at least that is better, there is hope for an escape from troubles hereafter.)

Perhaps nowhere in the macrocosm of the poem do we find a better example of the contextuality of meaning, of the paradox of the so-called hermeneutic circle, of the manner in which the meaning of the whole can only be constructed out of parts whose meaning, in turn, we cannot fully grasp unless we already have some sense of the whole. How are we to read even that minute and protean particle γε, so laden with emotion, but what emotion is it? And is ἐλπωρή hope or is it resignation?

---

[22] Flacelière (1971: 20), in a paroxysm of romantic fervor, agrees: "C'est la fin de l'*Odyssée*, car la suite du chant XXIII et tout le chant XXIV sont manifestement des interpolations ajoutées au poème d'Homère, qui nous apparaît donc bien comme dédié, pour l'essentiel, a l'exaltation de la fidélité conjugale et du bonheur du couple." See also Kirk 1962: 248–49.

Penelope's πένθος is still ἀμέτρητον (19.512): her grief is still without a μέτρον, a term, a boundary to measure it, like her husband's πόνος, like the story itself (23.248–50):

> ὦ γύναι, οὐ γάρ πω πάντων ἐπὶ πείρατ' ἀέλθλων
> ἤλθομεν, ἀλλ' ἔτ' ὄπισθεν ἀμέτρητος πόνος ἔσται.

(Woman, we have not come to the end of all our troubles; the future still holds unmeasured hardship.)

Odysseus had been sent to Tiresias purportedly to learn the *metra keleuthou*, the measurable stages of his journey home. He learns instead of an *ametrētos ponos* that carries us out of the poem, preventing the mind from taking any final measure of the work, unless we import our own verisimilar sense of appropriateness. Odysseus, of all men, epitomizes that ability of the mind to take stock of the world and to plan in terms of that understanding (μῆτις, νόος). But in the action of the poem he is ultimately confronted by the incommensurability of that world, and of his position within it (πόνος), in response to which he can only endure. Wherefore the epithet much used of him, *polytlas* 'much-enduring,' which stands in balance to his other most often used epithets, *polymētis* 'limitless in cunning,' and *polymēchanos* '(the man) of many devices'. He must endure and so must the skillful Penelope. In the end, the world's incommensurability—the lesson of the tragic myth—is nowise diminished, but neither is a major theme of the *Märchen*, the versatility and resilience of mind in its endeavor to take the world's measure.[23]

E. M. Forster has said that, but for wedding bells and funeral bells, no storyteller would know how to conclude. Tiresias's prophecy is an obstacle to both kinds of conclusion, embedding itself in contrary environments to serve

---

[23] That lack of measurability turns up also in the case of Heracles, who speaks of his ὀϊζὺς ἀπειρεσίη in book 11, where, incidentally, the poem again has it both ways: there is a mortal εἴδωλον of Heracles among the shades in the underworld; the other part—αὐτὸς—dwells immortally with Hebe, eternal youth.

contrary functions. It comes at two key points in the plot, each time with an opposite function. In the dark realm of the shades in book 11, it softens the grim finality of death, nature's adamantine law, the δίκη βροτῶν, the message of the tragic myth voiced with curt eloquence by the ghost of Achilles. In book 23, it intrudes to embitter pleasure at its peak, to skew the trajectory drawn by the folktale between desire and its object, to trouble the dream of culture. Claude Lévi-Strauss has taught us that the primary if not exclusive function of what he calls myth is to mediate insoluble cultural conflicts and contradictions, especially that which sets culture in opposition to nature. The prophecy of Tiresias performs this function, particularly and in part by a syntactic ploy, the *until* clause, used as we have seen for situations of both certain and uncertain outcome. The result is, if not a practical repression of uncertainty, at least a blurring of the line that divides it from the category of certainty, permitting the narrative to cease if not to conclude.

In that it is empty of meaning in itself, a narrative unit "unmarked" as to outcome, poised between the tragic myth and the hopeful *Märchen*, yet capable of taking on either of their opposed meanings, Homer's treatment of Tiresias's forecast may be called prophecy "in the zero-degree." The "zero-degree" of a term is an "unmarked" aspect of that term: not a total absence, but a *significant absence*. As Roland Barthes says (1970: 77): "the zero-degree testifies to the power held by any system of signs, of creating meaning 'out of nothing': 'that language can be content with an opposition between something and nothing' (Saussure)." This fruitful concept was employed in phonology by Roman Jakobson, but it has since been applied profitably in other areas.[24] Lévi-Strauss's anthropological application of the concept to the notion of *mana* suggests

---

[24] Such as logic. See, for example, Destouches 1950: 73: "*A* est dans l'état zéro, c'est à dire, n'existe pas effectivement mais sous certaines conditions on peut le faire apparaître; en somme, potentialité d'existence."

its potential for resolving otherwise immobilizing contradictions in cultural systems:

> We see in *mana, Wakan, oranda* and other notions of the same type, the conscious expression of a semantic function, whose role is to permit symbolic thought to operate in spite of the contradiction which is proper to it. In this way are explained the apparently insoluble antinomies attached to this notion. . . . At one and the same time force and action, quality and state, substantive and verb, abstract and concrete, omnipresent and localized—*mana* is in effect all these things. But is it not precisely because it is none of these things that *mana* is a simple form, or more exactly, a symbol in the pure state, and therefore capable of becoming charged with any sort of symbolic content whatever? In the system of symbols constituted by all cosmologies, *mana* would be a *valeur symbolique zéro*, that is to say a sign marking the necessity of symbolic content supplementary to that with which the signified is already loaded, but which can take on any value required, provided only that this value still remain part of the available reserve and is not, as phonologists put it, a group-term. . . . It could almost be said that the function of notions like *mana* is to be opposed to the absence of signification, without entailing by itself any particular signification. (Lévi-Strauss 1950: xlix–l and note)

This is, I think, precisely the manner in which the Tiresias prophecy functions in the semantic universe of the *Odyssey*, sustaining a narrative threatened with fracture by the conflict of its ideological components, myth and *Märchen*.[25]

This way of reading the text generates a thought-provoking parallel between the audience/readers of the *Odyssey*,

---

[25] It is Schlovski especially who has suggested the application of the notion of the zero-degree to the study of narrative conclusions (1929: 73–74 = 68–69 in German translation). See also the brief discussion in Jameson (1972: 63–64). Less technical, but more provocative, is Kermode 1966.

who are left to complete the poem,[26] and the Phaeacian
audience listening to Odysseus's tale of Tiresias's prophecy. At that point in the narrative, some of the events of
the prophecy have been fulfilled while others lie in the future. And it is up to the Phaeacian audience to carry Tiresias's prophecy to its next stage by bringing Odysseus
home,[27] but at the risk of their own destruction, prophe-
sied by Nausithous some years before. Here is yet another
link between the two prophecies, the situation of their respective audiences, one outside the poem and one within
it, each faced with a prophecy that allows them an 'open'
response.

The relationship between the Phaeacian audience and
Odysseus's narrative is interesting, for it touches their lives
in a profound and serious sense that transcends mere "entertainment." Demodocus's narrative of Odysseus was, for
them, "entertainment," distanced as their lives were from
its subject. But Odysseus's story of Poseidon's enmity puts

[26] I am indebted to Dina Sherzer for pointing out a parallel in the narrative practice of the Kuna Indians. I quote from her oral comment on
an earlier version of this part of my argument (transcribed in Peradotto
1986: 457): "The literature on myth . . . often argues that the purpose of
myth in preliterate society, especially when the myth is performed in
some way, is to solve a particular problem in that society or offer a moral
or a message within that society. Now, in my research with the Kuna Indians I found that while this is true, in actual performance it is sometimes
the case that the performer does not solve the problem: that is, he presents the problem, but rather, in a series of metaphors within the myth,
leaves the interpretation open to the audience and often leaves quite contradictory interpretations open to the audience. . . . A truly clever performer can even end the myth with a moral which is still in a metaphor,
so that the ambiguous and contradictory interpretation is still there."

[27] It is noteworthy that, in the syntax of Odysseus's account of Tiresias's
prophecy, his return home on an alien ship, the only stage that depends
on a decision *already made* by the Phaeacians, is represented factually, in
the indicative mood (νεῖαι, 11.114), a rather striking departure from the
careful optatives that have been used up to this point (ἵχοισθε, 104, 111)
and in a general context dominated, as we have observed, by uncertainty
and conditionality. How much of this may we mark down to subtle rhetorical deviation by Odysseus rather than to verbatim citation of Tiresias's
"actual" words?

in a whole new light the Phaeacian decision to escort him home. Now their own future safety is implicated in that decision. If those who follow Aristarchus in condemning Nausithous's prophecy at 8.564ff. are less than convincing, they are right in seeing that these lines profoundly alter the tone of Odysseus's tale in books 9 through 12. Odysseus's tale-within-a-tale is of such a special kind that it does much more than simply fill us in on his adventures between Troy and Ogygia. It forces us to register that new information also in its effect on its fictional audience as a frightening alteration of the framework within which their decision to help Odysseus was made.[28] The guest they purpose to escort home is revealed as the special enemy of the god who has threatened them with catastrophe for just such actions. As if that were not enough, the dilemma unexpressed explicitly in the linguistic code is further underscored in the narrative code by two of Odysseus's adventures, one following the other in his account, each suggesting contradictory moral imperatives: the Cyclops episode and the Aeolus episode. On the one side, the punishment of Polyphemus underscores the danger attendant on ill treatment of suppliant strangers, a danger best expressed in gnomic form in the linguistic code by the swineherd Eumaeus (14.56–58):

> ξεῖν', οὔ μοι θέμις ἔστ', οὐδ' εἰ κακίων σέθεν ἔλθοι,
> ξεῖνον ἀτιμῆσαι. πρὸς γὰρ Διός εἰσιν ἅπαντες
> ξεῖνοί τε πτωχοί τε.

(Stranger, it is not right for me to treat a stranger shabbily, not even if a worse fellow than you were to come along. For it is from Zeus that all strangers and beggars come.)[29]

On the other side are the words with which Aeolus states in the linguistic code what is already implicit in the narrative code, that it is improper to assist a man whom the gods hate (10.73–75):

---

[28] For a more detailed study of this, see Peradotto 1974.
[29] Compare Nausicaa's comment, 6.207–8.

οὐ γάρ μοι θέμις ἐστὶ κομιζέμεν οὐδ' ἀποπέμπειν
ἄνδρα τόν, ὅς τε θεοῖσιν ἀπέχθηται μακάρεσσιν.
ἔρρ', ἐπεὶ ἀθανάτοισιν ἀπεχθόμενος τόδ' ἱκάνεις.

(It is not right for me to give aid and a fair send-off to a man
hated by the blessed gods. Get out of here! For you've come
here the object of immortal odium.)[30]

These contradictory principles have their counterpart in
the ambivalence of the Phaeacian *ethos*, at once proud of
its hospitality and more than ordinarily suspicious of out-
siders (7.32–33).[31]

This tense, more engaged, existential relationship between audience and tale raises some interesting questions,
among which is the Phaeacian attitude about the veracity
of Odysseus, and the kind of person he represents himself
as being in comparison with what the name "Odysseus" refers to in the tales Demodocus has told. These questions
loom all the larger inasmuch as Odysseus, in finally dis-
closing his name, had attached to it preeminence among
all men in *dolos* 'trickery,' and his tale of himself makes
much of his *mētis* 'cunning intelligence.' In Alcinous's com-
pliment to Odysseus's narrative skill, he adverts to the
ever-lurking possibility of deception, if only politely to dismiss it in the case of his guest (11.363–66):

ὦ 'Οδυσεῦ, τὸ μὲν οὔ τί σ' ἐΐσκομεν εἰσορόωντες
ἠπεροπῆά τ' ἔμεν καὶ ἐπίκλοπον, οἷά τε πολλοὺς
βόσκει γαῖα μέλαινα πολυσπερέας ἀνθρώπους
ψεύδεά τ' ἀρτύνοντας, ὅθεν κέ τις οὐδὲ ἴδοιτο.

(You do not seem to us a beguiler and deceiver such as in
their scattered numbers the dark earth rears, fashioning
their fictions out of things no man could ever see to verify.)

---

[30] Cf. Levy (1963) who argues that the *Odyssey* generally shows traces of
two different cultural traditions in the area of host-guest relationships:
one a lavish aristocratic, courtly tradition, and the other a tradition of
impoverished peasants who cannot afford not to distrust strangers.

[31] On the second of these characteristics, one all too insufficiently appreciated in Homeric criticism, see Finley 1978: 100–101; Kakridis 1963:
88; and G. Rose 1969.

What Alcinous seems lightly to dismiss, the vexed relationship between a narrative and what it may refer to, is indeed a complicated question. What this man who names himself "Odysseus" claims of himself is largely out of sight, beyond the possibility of verification. Is this the same subject referred to by the name "Odysseus" in Demodocus's tales of Troy? Back in Ithaca, Telemachus too has heard the name of Odysseus, but for him what does it refer to, unless to the tales he has heard of the father he has never seen? And how trustworthy are those tales in a world so full of beguilers and deceivers, fashioning their fictions out of things no man could ever see to verify? Penelope will confront a man who names himself Odysseus, who looks like the husband she has not seen for twenty years. Does the name refer to the same person? Can she trust even to sight in a world where gods can take any mortal shape they choose? And what about the audience of the *Odyssey*, or its readers? What audience? What readers? For them what does the name "Odysseus" refer to? Does the name "Odysseus" refer to the "same" subject for a reader of, say, Homer, Sophocles, Euripides, Virgil, Dante, Tennyson (see Howell 1979)? If it does, how, for instance, does such a reader deal logically with an "identical" character who both does and does not perish before returning home from Troy (e.g., in Dante by contrast to Homer)? What is it precisely that *any* name refers to? The answer, which is very closely associated to the processes whereby literary texts are produced and received, is not as simple as at first sight it might seem. What follows is a stab at an answer.

Chapter 4

POLYTROPOS: THE NAMING OF THE SUBJECT

I am become a name.
—Tennyson, "Ulysses"

It is difficult to escape the conclusion that person-deixis in any language that manifests it (and, as far as we know, all natural languages do) is something that cannot be analysed away in terms of anything else. Deixis, in general, sets limits upon the possibility of decontextualization; and person-deixis, like certain kinds of modality, introduces an ineradicable subjectivity into the semantic structure of natural languages.
—John Lyons, *Semantics*

IT WOULD BE a rare study of the *Odyssey* that did not devote substantial attention to the names in the text, chief among them, of course, the name of its hero. The story of how Odysseus gets his name is framed suggestively within the tale of his rite of passage to manhood, the bloody boar hunt on Parnassus with his uncles, sons of Autolycus, arch-trickster and fast dealer in ambiguous speech, this tale itself framed by the larger narrative of how the long-lost hero is recognized by the one person, Eurycleia, who best knows what the name "Odysseus" refers to. The bibliography on the poem suggests that an essay on the name of Odysseus virtually functions as a scholarly rite of passage to *Odyssey* studies. This emphasis is not misplaced, for nowhere does Homeric and Hesiodic poetry, but especially the *Odyssey*, seem to be more self-conscious about language and its relation to things than when it comes to proper names. So it is not only our contemporary perspective, ineradicably preoccupied with language as it is, that puts this matter into such sharp focus. What is of interest from the contemporary perspective is the hardly accidental fact that there may be no more hotly debated issue in theoretical linguistics, learning theory, and philosophy of language than the problematical character of proper names. In short, where the ancient texts come closest to what we would call a discursive, philosophical reflection on the referential status of language is precisely where modern theoreticians are most divided: the status of proper names.

Near the end of book 8 of the *Odyssey*, the Phaeacian king Alcinous finally brings himself to ask Odysseus his name (8.550–54):

> εἴπ' ὄνομ' ὅττι σε κεῖθι κάλεον μήτηρ τε πατήρ τε,
> ἄλλοι θ' οἵ κατὰ ἄστυ καὶ οἳ περιναιετάουσιν.
> οὐ μὲν γάρ τις πάμπαν ἀνώνυμός ἐστ' ἀνθρώπων,
> οὐ κακὸς οὐδὲ μὲν ἐσθλός, ἐπὴν τὰ πρῶτα γένηται,
> ἀλλ' ἐπὶ πᾶσι τίθενται, ἐπεί κε τέκωσι, τοκῆες.

> (Tell me the name they call you by in your country, the one your mother and father use, and the townsmen and neighboring folk; for wholly nameless is no man, be he wretch or nobleman, from the time of his birth, but parents lay names on everyone whenever they bring them into the world.)

Many readers have read these words as "characteristically platitudinous" of Alcinous (Stanford 1965 *ad loc.*) or as the kind of broad truism we are supposed to excuse in Homeric poetry. But frequently, as the annals of anthropology remind us, the most familiar of our usages mask problems that most vigorously resist reflection. They "go without saying," or so we think. This is the case with proper names. J. R. Searle (1983: 231) has what must be the clearest formulation of the problem of proper names:

> We need to make repeated references to the same object, even when the object is not present, and so we give the object

a name. Henceforward this name is used to refer to that object. However, puzzles arise when we reflect on the following sorts of considerations: objects are not given to us prior to our system of representation; what counts as one object or the same object is a function of how we divide up the world. The world does not come to us already divided up into objects; we have to divide it; and how we divide it is up to our system of representation, and in that sense is up to us, even though the system is biologically, culturally, and linguistically shaped. Furthermore, in order that someone can give a name to a certain object or know that a name is the name of that object, he has to have some *other* representation of that object independently of just having the name.

In the history of dealing with this problem, which is coterminous with the history of western philosophy itself, one finds two opposing perspectives. One is the "no-sense" theory, perhaps the most widely accepted in modern philosophical discussions of the issue (Lyons 1968: 219). For John Stuart Mill, its most notable proponent, proper names are essentially meaningless; they simply stand for objects. In an argument that uses the terms "denotation" and "connotation" in specialized senses somewhat unfamiliar to nonspecialists, he reasons that while common nouns have both denotation and connotation, proper names have only denotation.[1] The common noun "horse," for example, *denotes* all horses and *connotes* all those properties which would figure in a definition of the word "horse." A proper name, by contrast, merely denotes the name bearer, but suggests no set of characteristics that could be used to distinguish the name bearer from other objects. This way of understanding proper names, discernible as early as Plato's *Theaetetus*, is essentially the same espoused

---

[1] John Stuart Mill, *A System of Logic*, bk. 1, ch. 2, esp. section 5. Denotation/connotation here are roughly equivalent to the terms "extension"/"intention" in the logic of classes, nearly opposite the meaning they have in less technical but perhaps more familiar literary terminology (Lyons 1968: 158–59, 207; and compare Barthes 1974: 6ff.).

by Wittgenstein and Russell. But largely because of the logical embarrassments generated by this theory when it has to account for proper names in informative identity statements and in existential statements, it was most vigorously opposed by Gottlob Frege, the chief exponent of what has been called the "sense and reference" theory. Here there is an insistence that names have meaning and even, in an uncommon and extreme formulation of the theory—Jespersen's—that a name is the most meaningful of words, expressing the totality of its *designatum*. Frege argued that the name must contain a sense in virtue of which and only in virtue of which it refers to an object. Without a sense to provide a "mode of presentation" (*Art des Gegebenseins*), we could not know to what the name referred. Searle summarizes our apparent dilemma in the face of such antagonistic explanations (1967: 488):

> According to the classical theory, names, if they are really names, necessarily have a reference and no sense at all. According to the Fregean theory, they essentially have a sense and only contingently have a reference. They refer if and only if there is an object which satisfies their sense. In the first theory proper names are *sui generis*, and indeed for Plato (in the *Theaetetus*) and Wittgenstein (in the *Tractatus*) they are the special connecting link between words and world; in the second theory proper names are only a species of disguised definite descriptions: every one is equivalent in meaning to a definite description which gives an explicit formulation of its sense. According to the first theory, naming is prior to describing; according to the second, describing is prior to naming, for a name only names by describing the object it names.

In short, how can you describe unless you have named the subject of description? On the other hand, how can you use a name that does not imply a description that would explain the name in existential contexts ("Odysseus never existed"), identity contexts ("This beggar is Odysseus"), and opaque contexts ("Who or what is Odysseus?")?

A tense compromise between such radical oppositions is possible. We must accept Mill's argument that a name does not tie us to any *particular* description, that, by definition, it can have no definition. With Frege, we must also assume that a name, or for that matter any singular term, must have a "mode of presentation," which is to say a certain kind of sense, as long as we do not follow him in taking for a definition the "identifying description" that can be substituted for the name. Again, Searle (1967: 491):

> We have the institution of proper names to perform the speech act of reference. The existence of these expressions derives from our need to separate the referring from the describing functions of language. But reference never occurs in complete isolation from description, for without some description, reference would be altogether impossible.

Without involving ourselves in too much more intricate logical detail, we should not leave this theoretical excursus without at least adverting to an important refinement in this compromise position, one that emphasizes the social contextuality of naming. The "identifying description" for a name is a group phenomenon. Gareth Evans (1977) expresses this version of the "description theory" when he argues that "associated with each name as used by a group of speakers who believe and intend that they are using the name with the same denotation, is a description or set of descriptions cullable from their beliefs which an item has to satisfy to be the bearer of the name." This means that it is not necessary that this description figure in *every* user's name-associated cluster, nor is it even likely to do so. Kripke would refine this yet further by adding a temporal dimension to the social, spacial configuration of the identifying description. He would require that a speaker's use of a name "will denote an item *x* if there is a causal chain of *reference-preserving links* leading back from his use on that occasion ultimately to the item *x* itself being involved in a name-acquiring transaction such as an explicit dubbing or the more gradual process whereby nicknames stick" (Evans 1977: 197). The importance of this insistence on the social contextuality of the name will become much clearer later when we concentrate our attention on the name of Odysseus.

If this discussion of the theory of proper names has taken us momentarily away from the *Odyssey*, it is only to provide us with a fresh perspective, a realignment of vision, a heightened alertness to capture what is likely to evade us. Nothing is more resistant to reflection than the familiar, and what is more familiar (quite literally even) than the use of names? What initially prompted this theoretical excursus was the poem's own intense interest in names. But there is more to it than that. The process of naming or of coming to recognize a name turns out to be intimately associated with the production of narrative and with the process of reading narrative (Barthes 1974: 92).

It has been the tendency of classical philology to encourage us to approach the *Odyssey* as a poem designed for an audience that already "knows" Odysseus. This notion of an "original audience" has grown irksome for many reasons, not least of which is that, despite its emptiness of content, its lack of specifying detail, and its consequent imperviousness to affirmation or denial, it is yet proposed as an authoritative ideal against which our readings of the text are to be evaluated. It is in short a domineering ghost whose power lies precisely in its absence.

But let me put those reservations aside for the moment and assume the perspective I have just impugned: that the poem is designed for an audience that already "knows" Odysseus. In what does this prior knowledge consist? To what does the name "Odysseus" refer? It obviously must have its source in other tales, which for us are not, except in small part, recoverable. But even if we had them and they were uniform in their representation of Odysseus's "character," the same question would have to be directed to them as to the *Odyssey* itself. In their absence, they are, as I said, minimally recoverable, and even then by processes of inference conditioned by our own purposes, by

our own questions addressed to the text. Some might infer, with Nagy and the more fundamentalist Parryites, a
more or less uniform and consistent tradition.[2] On the
other hand, it is at least as reasonable to assume that the
Odyssey had the effect of stabilizing a tradition characterized by inconsistency and plurality, of stabilizing, in effect,
a multiplicity in the denotation of Odysseus's name, the
way a historian's work might stabilize the multiplicity in the
interpretations of a particular figure or event, or the way
Hesiod appears to be trying to stabilize a polymorphous
and inconsistent theogonic tradition, in which divergent
narratives vie for something like canonical ideological
dominance. Herodotus seems to be reading his mythic
narrative tradition in this light when he attributes the character and form of the Greek pantheon largely to the work

---

[2] For Nagy (1979: 3), for example, what the poet means "is strictly reg-
ulated by tradition." "The poet," he argues, "has no intention of saying
anything untraditional." From Nagy's point of view (5), "the way to rec-
oncile the factor of formulaic composition with the factor of artistic unity
is to infer that both are a matter of tradition." Between this extreme statement of the matter and a romantic, mystical, equally unsatisfactory emphasis on individual artistic creation lies a reasonable balance, one that, I
believe, Nagy would agree is still consonant with his conception of tradition. Such a view is summarized by Lévi-Strauss (1966: 95) as follows:
"The sense in which infrastructures are primary is this: first, man is like
a player who, as he takes his place at the table, picks up cards which he
has not invented, for the cardgame is a datum of history and civilization.
Second, each deal is a result of a contingent distribution of the cards,
unknown to the players at the time. . . . We are well aware that different
players will not play the same game with the same hand even though the
rules set limits on the games that can be played with any given one." See
also Bourdieu 1977: 72–95, esp. 76: "To eliminate the need to resort to
'rules,' it would be necessary to establish in each case a complete description (which invocation of rules allows one to dispense with) of the relation
between the habitus, as a socially constituted system of cognitive and mo-
tivating structures, and the socially structured situation in which the
agents' *interests* are defined, and with them the objective functions and
subjective motivations of their practices. It would then become clear that,
as Weber indicated, the juridical and customary rule is never more than
a *secondary principle* of the determination of practices, intervening when
the primary principle, interest, fails." See also de Certeau 1984.

of Homer and Hesiod. We are encouraged in this view by the *Odyssey*'s deliberate silence (if suppression is not a better word) when it comes to those of Odysseus's unflattering characteristics and acts which, though they surface more conspicuously later in Greek literary evidence, are more at home in more primitive tales of a trickster-type out of which Homer's urbane and civilized Odysseus can readily be inferred to have developed.

The suppression of Odysseus's name in the proem has had no end of comment. There are, of course, other places in the text where that name is suppressed and for a much longer duration. In book 5, Hermes conveys to Calypso Zeus's will regarding Odysseus, but in their 53-line conversation, the hero's name is not mentioned. Hermes refers to him as ὀϊζυρώτατον ἄλλων (105), and on Calypso's tongue he is mere generic man (βροτὸν ἄνδρα, 129), humbled in reference by a series of eight pronouns (τὸν, 130, 134–35, μιν, 139–40, 142; οἱ, 143; ἣν, 144). In book 14, Eumaeus talks about Odysseus for 52 lines without using his name, and in response to disguised Odysseus's tactful query, remains evasive for yet another 22 lines before it finally comes out in line 144 (see Austin 1972). And for three whole books the visitor in Scheria is nameless, until pressed beyond evasion by the Phaeacian king. By contrast, the proem's 20-line delay seems brief, and yet it is far more expressive, for here it is *our* expectations, *our* need to know that are at issue, not those of some character in the story. The silence of the proem is really a sophisticated, more explicit realization of what would in fact be the case even if the name had been mentioned, as Achilles's is in the opening of the *Iliad*. Before being supplied with a "character," a "personality," what the linguist would call an "identifying description," what Barthes (1974: 94) would call a "figure" ("an impersonal network of symbols combined under the proper name"), the name would be inflated currency, an instrument of questionable exchange value, or in Searle's terms, an attempt at denotation without description. The least inflated currency, the currency with most exchange value, would be the name that, in addition to *reference*, bears a *sense* (like Frege's "evening star"), which obviates the need for an identifying description, because it supplies information about its referent that *is* identifying description. Except where arbitrary (e.g., a horse named Evening Star), such a name is its own identifying description; the name is identical to the story, or part of the story, of the name-bearer—its condensed, economic counter.

It is perhaps easier to see the point here by observing the case of Calypso. Unlike Odysseus, there is much, not least of all her name, to suggest that her personality owes more to this monumental poem than to the tradition, if in fact she is not wholly the creation of this poem.[3] Hers is a significant name. Unlike the name of Odysseus, which at least thus far in the poem has a reference but no sense, Calypso's name bears a sense sufficient to mark her role in the poem, a condensed token that, at the level of reading or listening, will seem to generate her story. This happens tersely at the first mention of her name (1.14), encapsulating in two or three lines her full story in book 5, to assure us that the name is not arbitrary.

The sense of her name embraces a semantic field constituted by an English-speaker's notions of "covering," "enfolding," "enveloping," "concealing," "placing or holding (something) in a center" or "hollow" or "enclosure" or "behind or under a surface," "protecting," "obliterating." Surrounding her name in 1.14 are expressions that fall within that same semantic field:

νύμφη πότνι᾽ ἔρυκε Καλυψώ, δῖα θεάων,
ἐν σπέσσι γλαφυροῖσι, λιλαιομένη πόσιν εἶναι.

She was "*holding him back* in her *hollow caverns*." (That, incidentally, will become the formula used by Odysseus sum-

---

[3] Parenthetically, I would argue that, from a functional point of view, she clearly cannot be understood apart from the narrative demand for a delay in Odysseus's return required to coincide with Telemachus's maturation.

marizing his encounter with her in retrospect, 9.29 and
23.334.) When, very shortly, the narrative returns to her,
her identifying description enlarges to set her at once in
the social context of the mythic tradition by the standard
device of naming a parent (Ἄτλαντος θυγάτηρ⁴), but her
name continues to specify her activity (κατερύκει), and
even to engender semantically homologous geography:
she lives "on a *wave-girt* island in the very *center* of the sea"
(literally its "navel"):

νήσῳ ἐν ἀμφιρύτῃ, ὅθι τ᾽ ὀμφαλός ἐστι θαλάσσης.

And finally, at the end of book 5, after the ravages of his
stormy return to pragmatic existence, as Odysseus with-
draws under the protective cover of the double olive-bush
and of sleep, the echo of the name returns to remind us of
the lady and the lot he has escaped (5.491–93):

ὣς Ὀδυσσεὺς φύλλοισι καλύψατο· τῷ δ᾽ ἄρ᾽ Ἀθήνη
ὕπνον ἐπ᾽ ὄμμασι χεῦ᾽, ἵνα μιν παύσειε τάχιστα
δυσπονέος καμάτοιο, φίλα βλέφαρ᾽ ἀμφικαλύψας.

(So Odysseus *enveloped* himself in leaves, and Athena poured
sleep upon his eyes, to help him find quick rest from painful
toil, *covering* his eyelids *over*.)

This relationship between a name and its analogous narrative can be characterized in rather more theoretical
terms by adopting the distinction that Todorov (1977: 240)
draws between "description" and "reading," a distinction
based upon a choice of particular methodological presuppositions. "For description," Todorov says,

⁴ Atlas's name and his epithet ὀλοόφρων belong roughly to the same semantic field and suggest perhaps the dangerous character inherited by
the daughter from her father. In fact, a textual variant for Ἄτλαντος
... θυγάτηρ ὀλοόφρονος is Ἄτλαντος θυγάτηρ ὀλοόφρων, possibly the
result of haplography (ΟΛΟΟΦΡΟΝΟΣ for ΟΛΟΟΦΡΟΝΟΣΟΣ [=
ὀλοόφρονος ὅς]). Also, it suggests that Calypso is, in her divine, genetic
relentlessness (τλα-), more than a match for her much-enduring (πολύτλας) captive.

the linguistic categories of a text are automatically pertinent
on the literary level, in the exact order of their organization
in the language. In its very course description follows the
stratification of the linguistic object: it proceeds from distinctive features to phonemes, from grammatical categories to
syntactic functions, from the rhythmic organization of the
line of verse to that of the strophe, and so on. Because of
this, all grammatical categories, for instance, will signify on
the same level, each in relation to the others. . . . Reading,
however, adopts another postulate: the literary work effects
a systematic short-circuiting of the autonomy of linguistic
levels. Here a grammatical form is made contiguous with a
certain theme of the text, the phonic or graphic constitution
of a proper noun will engender the remainder of the narrative.

To avoid misunderstanding, it should be reiterated that,
when we speak of Calypso's name as "generating" an aspect of her narrative, we mean that that is what *appears* to
be happening at the level of reading or listening, or, if you
will, on the syntagmatic plane. In reality, the relationship
between the name of Calypso and her activity and her geography is associative or paradigmatic. It is of absolutely
no interest to this type of analysis to speculate which came
first, the name of Calypso or her story, although it should
be fairly obvious that a name without a story is a name
without an identifying description, which is logically trou-
bling. A name without any identifying description, not
even a potentially knowable one, is not a name. When we
speak of an unfamiliar name, we mean the name of someone we do not know, whose story or part of whose story we
do not know, but could possibly know. So narratives do
seem to be logically prior to names, for narratives can and
do exist without names, while names cannot exist without
narratives from which an identifying description can be
drawn.

Gregory Nagy, in his study of the name of Achilles
(1976; 1979: 69–74), argues the historical priority of the

story over the name; *Akhilleus* (*'Αχί-λαϝος) is a "speaking name" fabricated to signify the central figure in a tale about a hero who brings distress, *akhos*, to the people, *lā-wos*. Most folktales, in fact, have merely functional names, like Calypso's, or none at all: Cinderella, Little Red Riding Hood, Oedipus, Hippolytus, The Fisherman and his Wife, the Frog King. In this they are very much like the contemporary analysis that is done on them, relying as it does on abstract functions to designate "characters": Propp's hero, villain, helper; Greimas's *actant, opposant, adjuvant*; Bremond's *patient, agent, influenceur, améliorateur, dégradateur*; and the like. The same kind of thing can be observed in Lévi-Strauss's much-discussed structural analysis of the Oedipus myth, in the fourth column of which are nothing but the names of the three dynasts—Labdacus, Laius, and Oedipus—all three reducible, in his view, to the common function of autochthonous birth by their suggestion of difficulty in walking straight or standing upright. This phenomenon makes Frege's theory especially attractive, according to which all names once "made sense" in the way that "Evening Star" and "Morning Star" and "Calypso" make sense. In fact, it is precisely for significant names such as these that Frege's theory is not only attractive, but valid.

Calypso's name, then, is perhaps the clearest instance of the sense-bearing name. It has connotation, in Mill's meaning of the term. It is motivated, as opposed to being a merely arbitrary denotator. By contrast, there are many names that seem to be merely arbitrary, or at least the poem gives us no reason to think of them as significant, as etymologically relevant. Some neither have nor require an identifying description, for they have nothing more than a generic role in the story, as for example the suitors Agelaus, Eurynomus, Amphimedon, Demoptolemus, Peisander, Polybus. Though they have names, the narrative as such does not grace them with individuation. Metrical and other formal motivational considerations aside, these characters might as easily have been designated by some such phrase as "six of the suitors." Where characters play a sufficiently specific, individual role in the narrative, they need an identifying description, even if their names are not, as in the case of the suitors just mentioned, functionally significant. In this class we must, I believe, place such names as Aegisthus, Agamemnon, Athena, Poseidon. Their identifying description is supplied by a variety of means: patronymic or other genealogical reference, a cluster of epithets, terse narrative or description (e.g., "the Aethiopians, who dwell apart, at the outermost edges of mankind, some in the far east, others in the far west," 1.23–24; "Aegisthus, whom famous Orestes, Agamemnon's son, killed," 1.30), not to speak of what the poem might silently imply from the tradition.

Yet other names lie closer to the border between the motivated and the arbitrary, giving us less obvious or less redundant signals than in Calypso's case, but still opening the door to the kind of contextual speculation and judgment, the eye for likenesses and differences, that figures so prominently in the thing we call interpretation. Think of Telemachus. Does the poem invite us to connect the character or story of Telemachus to the etymology of his name, which was given him, so it is said, because his father was going to be a "fighter far away" or a master bowman ("one who fights from a distance")?[5] At the poem's first mention of his name (1.113ff.), the immediate context suggests both his father's character as a warrior (σκέδασιν . . . θείη) and his distance from home (ποθεν ἐλθὼν):

> ὀσσόμενος πατέρ᾽ ἐσθλὸν ἐνὶ φρεσίν, εἴ ποθεν ἐλθὼν
> μνηστήρων τῶν μὲν σκέδασιν κατὰ δώματα θείη.

(. . . pondering in his mind's eye whether his noble father would come from wherever he was and scatter the suitors all over the house.)

---

[5] For a more detailed discussion of the practice of naming children for some characteristic or condition of a parent, see below, pp. 108, 134–38 and 164–65.

As for the other meaning of "Tele-machos," is it too much to see a relationship between Telemachus's name and the point near the climax of the second half of the poem (21.126–129) when the son will have to be quietly urged to abandon what would have been a successful attempt to string the bow of his father, all this coming at the end of a carefully orchestrated period of maturation in which the son moves from a state of aimless and powerless passivity to the confident and cunning pragmatism of his father?

Other names raise similar questions. Some of them as significant names bear but a thin functional relationship to the narrative, like those of all but a few of the Phaeacians, referring as they do to some aspect of their skill in sea-craft: Acroneos, Ocyalus, Elatreus, Nauteus, Prumneus, Anchialus, Eretmeus, Nausicaa. But what of a name like Elpenor? Has his name been fashioned in the likeness of his fate? The youngest of Odysseus's men and without much in the way of martial prowess or wits, doomed by heavy drink and forgetfulness to break his neck in a fall from Circe's rooftop, is he not truly Elp-enor, "the man of delusion"? The name of Antinous, chief villain among the suitors, deceitful "enemy of discernment" (*noos*),[6] has hardly been chosen arbitrarily by the poet, though parents would normally give such a name to mean "outstanding in discernment." Similarly, it is hard not to see in Eumaeus's name the economic token of his function in the narrative: with firm and sceptical gentleness to feed and protect the unknown wanderer, to play the nurse to the master he thinks long since lost. Unlike Eumaeus's name, on which both the scientific etymologist and poetic etymologist are likely to agree, Penelope's name is one of those instances where a Barthian literary reading will depart from a strictly "scientific" reading. For while the latter will resist any source of derivation other than πηνέλωψ (a kind of waterfowl),[7] the poetic reading will refuse to see mere coin-

---

[6] Athenaeus 15.677 supports "deceitful" as a meaning of the name.

[7] See, for example, Chantraine 1968–80 s.v. Πηνελόπεια: "Sûrement

cidence in the relationship between her action in the story and the words πήνη, meaning "woof," and λώπη, meaning "covering" or "robe." As in Calypso's case, the name seems to have generated the story of her ruse at the loom, whereas, what is more likely, it is a name designed for the heroine of just such a story.

Or take the name of Arete. To many scholarly readers of the text, it has hardly seemed coincidental that someone with such a name should be the object of Odysseus's supplications, that Nausicaa should explicitly direct Odysseus to bypass the king and bring his pleas to Arete, "the object of prayer." Such a reading, however, would have to deal with a rather serious objection: that nowhere else is this root used of prayers directed to any but divine beings.[8] If we accept the more likely meaning "she who is prayed for" (as *Désirée*), then we must consider the name arbitrary in relation to the narrative. But there is yet another and more interesting possibility. At the first mention of her name in the story, we are given an extensive genealogical excursus in which we learn that Alcinous's brother Rhexenor died without male issue "*while still a bridegroom*" in his house, leaving behind one daughter only, Arete" (7.65–67):

> τὸν μὲν ἄκουρον ἐόντα βάλ᾽ ἀργυρότοξος Ἀπόλλων
> νυμφίον ἐν μεγάρῳ, μίαν οἴην παῖδα λιπόντα
> Ἀρήτην.

The word νυμφίον makes it not unlikely that Arete was born *after* the untimely death of her father, and furthermore that she was named "Accursed" for his unhappy fate. It is not uncommon in many cultures, among them the society represented in Greek mythic and epic tradition, to name children for some untoward or disagreeable condition of a parent or other relative. We shall have reason to

---

tiré de πηνέλωψ (Solmsen, *KZ* 42, 1908, 232), comme Μερόπη de μέρωψ. . . . Toutes les autres explications de Πηνελόπεια sont ruineuses."

[8] *Lexikon des Frügreichischen Epos* (hereafter *LfgrE*) s.v. ἀράομαι.

examine this phenomenon in greater detail later, when we
come to the naming of Odysseus himself.

Still another variation in naming motivation is illustrated
by the name of Idomeneus: the generation of a minor narrative incident or theme out of a name already probably
long identified by some more important narrative or series
of narratives. In the section of the *Eoiai* devoted to the
suitors of Helen (fr. 204.56–63 Merkelbach and West) the
following is devoted to Idomeneus:

> ἐκ Κρήτης δ' ἐμνᾶτο μέγα σθένος Ἰδομ[ενῆος
> Δευκαλίδης, Μίνωος ἀγακλειτοῖο γενέ[θλης·
> οὐδέ τινα μνηστῆρα μ[ε]τάγγελον ἄλλ[ον ἔπεμψεν,
> ἀλλ' αὐτὸς [σ]ὺν νηῒ πολυκλήϊδι μελαίνη[ι
> βῆ ὑπὲρ Ὠγυλίου πόντου διὰ κῦμα κελαιν[ὸν
> Τυνδαρέου ποτὶ δῶμα δαΐφρονος, ὄφρ[α ἴδοιτο
> Ἀ]ρ[γείην] Ἑλένην, μηδ' ἄλλων οἷον ἀκ[ούοι
> μῦθον, ὅς] ἤδη πᾶσαν ἐπὶ [χθ]όνα δῖαν ἵκαν[εν
> . . . .

(And from Crete mighty Idomeneus wooed her, he the son
of Deucalion and offspring of famous Minos. And he sent
no proxy as suitor in his place, but came himself with his
black, many-benched ship over the Ogylian sea through the
dark wave to the house of shrewd Tyndareus *to see* Argive
Helen for himself, not merely *to hear* from others the *story*
that had already spread over all the land.)

Is it merely coincidental that, in a series of very brief vi-
gnettes allowing for little more than a genealogical reference, this particular distinctive feature—the desire to wit-
ness for oneself (ἴδοιτο) rather than trust to hearsay
(μῦθον)—should be associated with a character whose
name gives the appearance of containing the root for vision (Ἰδομενεύς)? It seems a lot less arbitrary when we
realize that the character comes from Crete, where traditionally little trust resides in μῦθος. Is there some connection between this and the fact that disguised Odysseus

chooses the court of Idomeneus as the site of his fictitious eyewitness account of Odysseus?[9]

It should be clear by now that seeing significance in many names is a matter of interpretation, and that audiences culturally inclined, as we are, to consider names arbitrary will approach the exercise with more scepticism than those whose cultural predisposition is recalcitrant to unintelligibility, and for whom either everything makes sense or nothing does.[10] Sometimes, as in the case of what

[9] It is Idomeneus also who, like Jephtha in *Judges* 11.30ff., vows to sacrifice to Poseidon whatever he first encounters on his return to Crete, only to find that it is his son (or, in another version, his daughter).

[10] See Lévi-Strauss 1966: 172–73. Concepts of the arbitrary, the accidental, the coincidental, are clearly the product of a philosophical and scientific understanding of the world, within which they cover those 'specific' and variable elements of an event which fall outside a set of general and invariable explanatory laws. On this point see Cassirer 1955: 43–49, esp. 47–48:

"The contrast between law and arbitrariness, necessity and contingency must be critically analyzed and more closely defined before it is applicable to the relation between mythical and scientific thought. . . . Inability to conceive of an event that is in any sense 'accidental' has, in any case, been called characteristic of mythical thinking. Often where *we* from the standpoint of science speak of 'accident,' mythical consciousness insists on a cause and in every single case postulates such a cause. . . . In this light, mythical thinking seems to be so far from an abritrary lawlessness that on the contrary we are tempted rather to speak of a kind of hypertrophy of the causal 'instinct' and of a need for causal explanation. Indeed, the proposition that nothing in the world happens by accident and everything by conscious purpose has sometimes been called fundamental to the mythical world view.

"Here again it is not the concept of causality as such but the specific form of causal explanation which underlies the difference and contrast between the two spiritual worlds. . . . Science is content if it succeeds in apprehending the individual event in space and time as a special instance of a general law but asks no further 'why' regarding the individualization as such, regarding the here and now. The mythical consciousness, on the other hand, applies its 'why' precisely to the particular and unique. It 'explains' the individual event by postulating individual acts of the will. Even though our causal concepts are directed toward the apprehension and specification of the particular, although in fulfilling this purpose they differentiate themselves and complement and determine one another, nevertheless they always leave a certain sphere of indeterminacy surrounding the particular. For precisely *as* concepts they cannot exhaust

has traditionally been called epexegesis, where an etymologically synonymous expression stands in proximity to a name, the connection is too obvious and deliberate to be discounted. So, for example, the Phaeacian bard Demodocus (δῆμος, δοκέω), whose name seems already to be motivated dramatically in the narrative by the special deference given him, is also explicitly described in an epithet as "honored by the people" (Δημόδοκος, λαοῖσι τετιμένος, 13.28; compare 8.472). Even more obvious are instances of paronomasia, as when the narrator, after showing us the father of slain Antinous, Eupeithes, in his attempt to persuade (πειθ-) the suitors' relatives to vengeance, goes on to use a play on words to comment on his partial success (24.465): Εὐπείθει πείθοντ᾽ ("they were persuaded by 'Good-Persuader' "). Other cases are not so obvious. Take the name of Alcinous. It is not so easy to see either ἀλκή or νόος as functions he prominently exercises in the narrative. On the other hand, it cannot be accidental (i.e., arbitrary) that most of the formulaic expressions containing his name express either power or intelligence: κρεῖον (8.382 et al.), θεῶν ἄπο μήδεα εἰδώς (6.12), δαΐφρονος (8.8 et al.), μένος (7.176 et al.), μεγαλήτορος (6.17 et al.), θεοειδής (7.231) (Sulzberger 1926: 383–84).

The name of Odysseus's dog Argus presents us with a simple but interesting variation on the type of linguistic motivation observable in the name of Calypso. The name has about the same semantic range as English "Flash," suggesting both swiftness and brightness of appearance. Inasmuch as it appears to have been a common epithet of dogs (κύνες ἀργοί, 2.11, 17.52, 20.145), we might have simply assumed that poor Argus's name displays no more

concrete-intuitive existence and events; they cannot exhaust all the countless 'modifications' of the general rule, which may occur at any particular time. Here every particular is indeed subject to the universal but cannot be fully deduced from it alone. Even the 'special laws of nature' represent something new and specific as opposed to the general principle, the principle of causality as such. They are subject to this principle; they fall *under* it, but in their concrete formulation they are not postulated *by* it and they cannot be determined by it alone."

than merely generic motivation (like the unfortunate son of Priam named Δῖος—or is it Ἄγαυος [ΔΙΟΝ ΑΓΑ-ΥΟΝ, *Il.* 24.251]? The scholiasts can't agree!). But that seems to be ruled out by the deliberate way in which the narrative, as in Calypso's case, engenders associative or paradigmatic equivalents for the name, almost as if the name were itself generating the narrative, as it indeed appears to be doing at the level of performance. We hear of Argus from three voices: the narrator, Odysseus, and Eumaeus. Each comments, one way or another, on the animal's speed and complexion. In the very first line of the Argus vignette (17.291–327), the narrator sets the tone:

ἂν δέ κύων κεφαλήν τε καὶ οὔατα <u>κείμενος</u> ἔσχεν.

(*Though lying still*, the dog raised his head and ears.)

Unlike the dogs who make a quick rush for (ἐπέδραμον) Odysseus at sight in book 14, Argus the swift is immobilized—κείμενος—a verbal root that occurs three times in the first ten lines of the narrator's remarks to characterize the animal (κεῖτ᾽ ἀπόθεστος, 17.296; ἔνθα κύων κεῖτ᾽ Ἄργος, 17.300); so immobilized is he that he is wholly unable to approach his master (303–4):

ἆσσον δ᾽ οὐκέτ᾽ ἔπειτα δυνήσατο οἷο ἄνακτος
ἐλθέμεν.

Furthermore, any brightness there once was in his coat is dimmed by the filth he lies in (ἐν πολλῇ κόπρῳ, 297). Odysseus queries Eumaeus about the dog, in his opening line using what now seems the code word for Argus's condition—*keit'(o)*—and then proceeding to comment on his complexion and to speculate on his former speed (306–10):

Εὔμαι᾽, ἦ μάλα θαῦμα κύων ὅδε κεῖτ᾽ ἐνι κόπρῳ.
καλὸς μὲν δέμας ἐστίν, ἀτὰρ τόδε γ᾽ οὐ σάφα οἶδα
ἦ δὴ καὶ τραχὺς ἔσκε θέειν ἐπὶ εἴδεϊ τῷδε,
ἦ αὔτως οἷοί τε τραπεζῆες κύνες ἀνδρῶν
γίγνοντ᾽, ἀγλαΐης δ᾽ ἕνεκεν κομέουσιν ἄνακτες.

(Eumaeus, I'm really quite surprised that this dog is left to lie here in the dung; from the look of him [*demas*], he's of a good breed, but it's hard for me to tell whether he had speed to match his looks, or whether he was just one of those table dogs kings keep for show.)

Such dogs, Odysseus says, are kept for pomp or show, as an ornament (ἀγλαΐη), a word in the same semantic field as ἀργός, suggesting brightness or splendor. Eumaeus in his turn responds by reminiscing on the dog's former complexion (δέμας, 313) and speed (ταχυτῆτα, 315), and ends by lamenting the wretched fate in which Argus is *held fast* (νῦν δ᾽ ἔχεται κακότητι, 318). The narrator rounds out the sad account with the death of the dog, expressed in a phrase wholly appropriate to the consistent pattern we have observed: it is the "destiny of *black* death" that finally catches up with bright Argus (326):

Ἄργον δ᾽ αὖ κατὰ μοῖρ᾽ ἔλαβεν μέλανος θανάτοιο.

If one tries to imagine this story with an arbitrary name in place of "Argus," it becomes clear how effectual the relationship between the name "Argus" and the construction of the narrative is. Without question there would still remain the pathos of a scene in which the master and his dog are reunited after twenty years, the one forced by the need for disguise to mask his true feeling, the other straining to give a weak sign of recognition before he dies. But the irony would be gone from such a version, and the concentration on the animal's former speed and splendor would be comparatively fortuitous. In short, the name would not condense and recapitulate the narrative. Also, the irony that we find in the actual account should alert us to a not always obvious corollary of naming motivation, that such motivation is provided not only by the positive meaning of a term, but also by such terms as are logically presupposed by it in what was traditionally called the logical square of oppositions lying at the heart of Greimas's "modèle constitutionnel" of meaning. In other words, a name can be as securely motivated by its contrary or contradictory as by its positive sense. To name a dwarf "Goliath" is as surely motivated as to name him "Shorty," and both names are motivated in a way that such a name as "Jim" is not.

We have been talking at length about so-called significant names—names that are not arbitrary, but that contain a *sense* in addition to a *reference*, and that in effect supply their own identifying description. In all this discussion, we should be careful to keep the concept of identifying description separate from that of sense. An identifying description can be achieved in a variety of ways, by a genealogy, for example, or by narrative arbitrarily related to the literal sense of the name. The significant name is the most economical way of achieving an identifying description, for the latter is identical to the literal sense of the name. In short, significant names obliterate the distinction between sense and reference.

This long excursus on significant names interrupted and deferred our discussion of the suppression of Odysseus's name in the proem, to which we must now return. What we find there is unusual: not only does no name appear in the first line to tell us whose story this is, but there is no unequivocal sign that Odysseus is its subject until the mention of Ithaca in line 18, leading up to his actual name in line 21. Formally, the opening of the *Odyssey* is a process of defamiliarization that results in a sharpening and refocusing of attention along untraditional lines, even in an audience for whom the identity of its subject is not a literal mystery, an audience that is not encountering the poem for the first time or that has been supplied with such an extratextual clue as a title ("the Odyssey"). In other words, the absence of a name here is likely to have been so startling to the expectations created by traditional practice that, but for the first word in the poem, *andra*, we would be programmed to take *polytropon* as a proper name. By contrast, the *Iliad* names its hero immediately and sets him in a social context with his patronymic. And if we follow Palmer (1963a: 79) and Nagy (1979: 69–74) in reading Akhilleus as *Akhi-lāwos* ("whose *lāwos* has *akhos*," or "he who

has the host of fighting men grieving"), the very next line
of the poem supplies, as in Calypso's case, an instant epexegesis on the name, summing up the role its bearer will
play in the narrative about to unfold, the tale of his de-
structive wrath, which "laid on the Achaeans woes without
number" (*myri' Achaiois alge' ethēken*), and even suggestively
deriving the name of the Achaeans from the *akhos* or woe
they bear (Nagy 1979: 83–93).

The *Odyssey* displays a similar technique, but instead of a
name it targets the epithet *polytropos* for epexegetic play.
The deliberateness and redundancy with which this is accomplished should surely convince even those sceptical
readers disinclined to find Palmer's etymology of *Akhilleus*
sufficiently undisguised to be functional in *Iliad* 1.1. The
word chosen to characterize the yet unknown hero of the
poem in lieu of his name is a rich and unstable ambiguity.
Taken in an active sense *polytropos* literally means "(a person) of many turns," and suggests the semantic range em-
braced by such English expressions as "infinitely clever,"
"versatile," "shifty," "complex," "of many guises" or "disguises," "of changeable" or "exchangeable character."
Taken in a passive sense it suggests "turned in many direc-
tions," "much travelled," even "much buffetted."[11] The
word *polytropos* triggers what I have called epexegetic play
to underscore its senses, alternately active and passive, of
versatility, transition, and plurality. This *polytropos*, we are
told, was *forced to wander* (*planchthē*, 2) very *much* (*polla*, 1);
he saw the cities and knew the minds of *many* (*pollōn*, 3)
men, and he endured *many* (*polla*, 4) sufferings at sea.
Even *planchthē* is not unambiguously passive, as I have just
translated it, but yields, like so many Homeric aorist verbs
in -θην, a *middle* meaning, poised between the active voice
and the passive. In short, *polla planchthē* carries the same
ambiguity as *polytropos*, articulating at the very outset of the

---

[11] A well-attested variant reading, πολύκροτον, from κρότος (a noise
made by beating or striking something), offers the same possibility of being read actively or passively.

poem a notion of character *in the middle voice*, between the purely active and the purely passive. This idea will be developed more fully in the next chapter.

Thus *polytropos* accomplishes the very opposite of a name, for instead of fixing its referent, as a name would, in an identifiable location within the social matrix or locking him into a narrative destiny manifest in the name, it suggests polymorphism, mutability, plurality, variability, transition, the crossing of borders, the wearing of masks, the assumption of multiple roles. It unsettles, elicits a mental activity that in the language of the poem is μερμηρί- ζειν, to be in a quandary. It is no accident that, in our extant evidence, the only other bearer of the epithet *polytropos* is the volatile divine crosser of borders, Hermes, great-grandfather of Odysseus. And our observations about the name of Calypso are further enriched in this context. For when she is introduced in the lines immediately following the proem, with our hero still unidentified, a powerful tension is introduced at the most fundamental of semantic levels between the ideas of constraint and freedom, for, as we have seen, that is precisely how the name Calypso stands in semantic opposition to *polytropos*. We might even venture to say that these two terms, placed in juxtaposition, give us the raw, almost cleanly abstract prerequisites for narrative as such: the subject capable of many moves is immobilized, the polymorph enveloped, the crosser of borders held in hollow caves, desire kept from its object.

In summary then, whereas the opening of the *Iliad* suggests a sense of destiny, of fatedness in the relationship it establishes between its hero's name and his life story, the *Odyssey* follows a stratagem of deferral, building a controlled identifying description prior to the name's disclosure, seemingly not satisfied to set the narrative in a traditional framework triggered by simple nomination or to fix too early or too firmly its hero's character and destiny by finding them in his name. In other words, instead of starting out "Sing, Goddess, the homecoming of Odysseus, son of Laertes" (*νόστον ἄειδε, Θεά, Λαεϱιάδεω 'Οδυσῆος), the poem sets out quite deliberately to create what Barthes (1974: 94) calls a *figure*, an anonymous and impersonal network of symbols, before attaching a proper name to it, thus making explicit what is merely implicit and masked in all naming. Moreover, the quick social identification by paternity so prominent elsewhere in the Homeric poems is here deferred for nearly 200 lines, and the formulaic patronym *Laertiadēs* does not occur until 5.203. The closest the proem comes to narrowing the range of inquiry it provokes is to place its subject among the surviving sackers of Troy.[12] In doing this, interestingly enough, the narrator acts exactly as Odysseus himself will be made to do when, in response to Polyphemus's first query about his identity (9.252–65), he merely locates himself generically and anonymously among the troops (*laoi*) of Agamemnon.

It was pointed out earlier that the name of Calypso and the terse epexegesis of it encapsulated the full narrative elaboration of book 5. In the same way, the proem of the *Odyssey* accomplishes in a short and compressed format the larger function of books 1 through 4. In fact, through the proem especially, but also through the rest of the first four books, the problem of nomination is there for the audience to confront as it accompanies Telemachus on his search for, not simply information about, but an identifying description of the father he knows literally only by name, which is to say not at all, since without an identifying description, that name or any name is useless. The formal features of this narrative invite the reader or audience to realize their common plight with Telemachus, some entering the text with more knowledge of its hero, some with

---

[12] On the other hand, we may have to concede that, with the expression *ptoliethron epersen*, "he sacked the city," the proem is offering a hint to an audience or reader sufficiently subtle to see an epithet, *ptoliporthos* (also -*ios*), used of Odysseus among others in the *Iliad*, and about to be used eight times in the *Odyssey* and exclusively of Odysseus. It is also the name of Odysseus's son by Penelope in the lost epic *Thesprotis*, according to Pausanias (8.12.5–6).

less, others perhaps with nothing but the name, like Telemachus, forced to conjure imaginary visions in his
mind's eye (ὀσσόμενος πατέρ᾽ ἐσθλὸν ἐνὶ φρεσίν, 1.115),
then bit by bit to shape a presumptive semblance of his
father out of the fragments of other people's memories,
before the climactic moment when, bolstered by the narratives gathered in his travels, he is urged by his father in
the flesh to accept him for *just such a man* as he has heard
about (16.204–5):

> οὐ μὲν γάρ τοι ἔτ᾽ ἄλλος ἐλεύσεται ἐνθάδ᾽ Ὀδυσσεύς,
> ἀλλ᾽ ὅδ᾽ ἐγὼ τοιόσδε. . . .

(No other Odysseus will ever come here,
But here am I just such a one as he.)

The process by which Telemachus comes to know his father and constantly to revise and adjust that knowledge is
none other than that by which any audience will have to
place this narrative into an intertextual context of other
narratives, its variable framework of verisimilitude, which
will include, among many other things, particularities such
as what kind of person Odysseus is, and generalities such
as what human beings can or are likely to do, what they
can expect at the gods' hands, and how the world is confi-
gured. The same control that Athena has exercised in di-
recting Telemachus's growing knowledge of his father, the
narrator exercises in shaping an identifying description
for the audience, with whatever predispositions it brings
to the transaction.

It is Athena also who, even before we are introduced to
Telemachus, is the vehicle for controlling any tendency an
audience might have to conjure inappropriate significance
out of Odysseus's name in relation to the adverse lot in
which we find him at the beginning of book 1. In the gath-
ering of the Olympians, Zeus has just propounded the thesis, discussed in Chapter 3, that human misery ὑπὲρ μόρον
("exceeding natural allotment") is more the result of ἀτασ-
θαλίαι ("moral recklessness") than of divine initiative

(1.32ff.). To this Athena responds with the case of suffering Odysseus—δυσμόρῳ—as counterevidence, punctuating
her remarks with the famous word-play on his name (62):
"Why do you find Odysseus so *odious, Zeus?*"

τί νύ οἱ τόσον <u>ὠδύσαο, Ζεῦ</u>;

To those who would, like Job's simplistic counsellors or
certain of the characters in the *Odyssey*, interpret Odysseus's condition simply as the product of Zeus's anger, the
text here offers, at least for the time being, a terse dis-
claimer. In the strongest possible terms Zeus himself denies any disaffection with Odysseus. The mortal's troubles
are indeed the result of anger, he says, but Poseidon's, not
his own. So immediately Zeus's principle as a touchstone
of human suffering seems to fall short of absolute validity,
and at least half of Athena's epexegesis is shown to fit: the
anger (*ὀδύσσομαι). The precise relationship between
Odysseus's name and anger will be more plainly laid bare,
but not until eighteen books later, after the character in its
full dimensionality has been displayed as a vigorous and
unstable dialectic between the ability actively to engage
and transform the world and the passive subjection to its
unalterable necessities, a dialectic between the characteristics signified by such terms as *polymētis, polymēchanos, poly-
phrōn, polykerdēs* and *ptoliporthos* on the one side and that
signified by *polytlas* on the other, an alteration in the long
run defined by the ambivalence within the single term *polytropos*. And to the extent that the world, as expressed by
the poem's "centripetal" voice, is understood to be ruled
by necessities—divine, social, political, it may be inevitable
that the unconventional urge to alter or evade them, expressed by a "centrifugal" voice, will incur hatred, that the
polytropos will be *odyssamenos*: "the man of hate." That will
be the theme of the next chapter.

Chapter 5

POLYARĒTOS: THE UNHALLOWED NAME OF ODYSSEUS

He is troubled by any *image* of himself, suffers when
he is named.
—Roland Barthes, *Roland Barthes*

The fact is I think I am a verb instead of a personal
pronoun. A verb is anything that signifies to be; to
do; or to suffer. I signify all three.
—Ulysses S. Grant's last recorded words

Nouns are for God and verbs for man.
—Milorad Pavić, *Dictionary of the Khazars*

IN THE MIDDLE of book 19, Penelope asks the disguised
stranger his name, parentage, and home country. He puts
her off, citing the pain such memories would rouse up.
When she persists, he calls himself Aithon, grandson of
king Minos, from Crete (again, the land of liars!), and
weaves a marvellous network of fiction out of things no
man could ever see to verify, yet so full of past reality and
the substance of her own desires that it draws her tears
and wins her trust. She orders the stranger's feet bathed
and, when he expresses reluctance to risk a young maidservant's ridicule, it is his old nurse Eurycleia who is called
to the task. In the midst of her work, she recognizes the
scar Odysseus received as a young man on a boar hunt
with his uncles, sons of Autolycus. That tale is told at some
length, becoming itself the frame for the story of a still earlier event, the naming of Odysseus.

This way of proceeding is so inimical to late classical and

modern (but not "postmodern") habits of reading, and to a prescriptive normativeness in critical practice among philologists, that it has had few admirers. If the author of the *Poetics* possessed a text with this passage in it, he has forgotten its place there (7.1451a), arguing that it lacks any necessary or plausible relation to what he considers the unified action of the *Odyssey*. Concurring in this judgment, many later critics would condemn 395–466 altogether as an interpolation. In a now famous essay, Erich Auerbach (1953: 1–20) is constrained to explain and to justify what in this passage appears to others as an "inappropriate" sense of perspective, or of foregrounding and backgrounding, by what he considers the basic impulse of Homeric style (ibid.: 4):

> to represent phenomena in a fully externalized form, visible and palpable in all their parts, and completely fixed in their spatial and temporal relations. . . . Like the separate phenomena themselves, their relationships—their temporal, local, causal, final, consecutive, comparative, concessive, antithetical, and conditional limitations—are brought to light in perfect fullness; so that a continuous rhythmic procession of phenomena passes by, and never is there a form left fragmentary or half-illuminated, never a lacuna, never a gap, never a glimpse of unplumbed depths.

However much this helps us to appreciate the differences between Homeric epic style and that of Old Testament narrative—for that after all is Auerbach's chief purpose—it remains incomplete as an explanation of the present passage. Without impugning Auerbach's essential insight, we may nonetheless insist that he overstates the case. The poet does not, in fact, treat with extensive foregrounding *everything* that falls within the purview of his story. Like every storyteller, he selects, and only a critical perspective tied to an epistemology of naive realism would fail to see this. Furthermore, even when the poet seems to concentrate on some detail considered arbitrary or inessential by later narrative and critical practice, he rarely deals with it at such length as here. In fact, Auerbach chooses to discuss this passage precisely because, in the class of such digressions, it seems to be the most extravagant.

Here is another instance, I would submit, where the distinction between motivation and function can help us. What we call motivation is restricted by verisimilitude, by a culturally relative normativeness. What is considered "appropriate" or "extravagant" in length, "essential" or "incidental" in details, what is considered a "digression" in the first place is all a matter of cultural variance. The same is true of the concept of character. If we insist on importing a conventional sense of psychological coherence or character consistency to our reading of this passage, then we shall be obliged to press our criticism of it still further. Otherwise, how could we fail to be troubled by the way in which Odysseus, the master of intelligence and cunning, is made to request an older maidservant in place of a younger one to wash his feet, without realizing who is likely to get the job! And then, after Eurycleia is ordered to her work, it is not until the water is actually poured that Odysseus *suddenly* realizes the obvious danger (αὐτίκα γὰρ κατὰ θυμὸν ὀίσατο, 390)! A character with the power to anticipate the incalculable in book 9 is here made to overlook the obvious. Is this "consistent" with the hero who is *polymētis*, a word used of him (should we now say ironically?) more often in this book than in any other—twelve times, eight of them in the passage leading up to this monumental improvidence?[1] Add some very curtly contrived divine machinery (τῇ γὰρ ᾽Αθηναίη νόον ἔτραπεν, 479):

---

[1] Compare another inconsistency: in book 8, at Demodocus's tales of Troy, Odysseus twice breaks down in fits of weeping too overwhelming to hide from Alcinous; but in book 17, at the sight of old Argus, he easily manages to hide a furtive tear from Eumaeus, and in book 19, before the wife he has not seen in twenty years, herself awash with tears, "he keeps his eyes fixed, like horn or iron, tears hidden by trickery" (19.211–12): ὀφθαλμοὶ δ᾽ ὡς εἰ κέρα᾽ ἕστασαν ἠὲ σίδηρος / ἀτρέμας ἐν βλεφάροισι· δόλῳ δ᾽ ὅ γε δάκρυα κεῦθεν. What accounts for these dramatically divergent responses has less to do with motivation derived from character or differences in the stimuli than with the functional goals to be achieved in the ensuing narrative.

the goddess of the many turns has turned Penelope's attention elsewhere to keep her deaf and blind to some very noisy goings-on no more than an arm's length away: Odysseus's foot falling into the washing pan, the loud clang of bronze (κανάχησε δὲ χαλκός, 469) as it overturns, spilling its contents, and the subsequent conversation between Eurycleia and Odysseus. Put all this together and the result will seem botched by standards of verisimilitude derived from the nineteenth-century novel by those who use the term "realism" as if its meaning were innocently unproblematical.[2] If we feel discomfort at all this, it may be our inappropriate expectations that require adjustment, not the text. And if that will not work, then perhaps we need to focus less on motivation in this passage than on its function.

On a superficial level, the scene serves to disclose Odysseus's identity to an absolutely trustworthy servant, well in advance of Penelope's recognition, for the advantage that may give him in the ensuing showdown with the suitors. But we surely cannot stop there. It can be argued that the recognition need not have taken place at this point, nor did it require the story of the scar, at least not a story at such length. But far and away the most telling objection is that the recognition would not require the story of Odysseus's naming. So the question of function here turns out to be more complex. If we are prepared to readjust our perspective to consider the story of Odysseus's naming not as a digression-within-a-digression, but as something at or near the center of attention in book 19, then the picture changes considerably. It well may be that the embedding process functions to establish a pseudo-causal relationship among elements from three separate narratives as if they were one, and in so doing reintroduces the grand theoretical question, the problem of human suffering, raised by Zeus early in book 1 almost as if it were a frame for the whole poem.

[2] On the problems associated with the term "realism," see especially Jakobson 1987: ch. 1.

The vignette of Odysseus's naming is introduced in such a way as to force a recall of Athena's punning reference to the name in 1.62. In the half-true lie that disguised Odysseus tells Penelope of his wanderings, he editorializes on the loss of his ship and crew off Thrinacia, using the same words that form Athena's pun (19.275–76):

> ὀδύσαντο γὰρ αὐτῷ
> Ζεὺς καὶ Ἥέλιος· τοῦ γὰρ βόας ἔκταν ἑταῖροι.

(They found him *odious*, Zeus and Helios, whose cattle his companions had killed.)

Shortly thereafter, that pun is paraphrased. As Eurycleia prepares for her task, she tearfully addresses the child (*teknon*) she thinks absent, but so general are her opening remarks that it takes several lines before we realize she is not intentionally addressing the stranger, which, unbeknown to her, is exactly what she *is* doing. She expresses the simple explanation for human suffering, the one rejected in book 1—the anger of Zeus—in words synonymous with Athena's pun on the name of Odysseus (363–64):

> ὤ μοι ἐγὼ σέο, τέκνον, ἀμήχανος· ἦ σε περὶ Ζεὺς
> ἀνθρώπων ἔχθαιρε θεουδέα θυμὸν ἔχοντα.

(Oh, how powerless I am to help you, child. Surely *Zeus hated* you beyond all men despite your piety.)

Back in book 1, Odysseus's sacrifices had been prominently featured in Athena's case against Zeus's theory of human suffering (1.61), and Zeus himself did not hesitate to admit Odysseus's preeminence among mortals in that regard (1.66–67). Here in book 19, Eurycleia makes the same case, but more strongly, to underscore the discrepancy between his piety and his treatment at the hands of the gods:

> οὐ γάρ πώ τις τόσσα βροτῶν Διὶ τερπικεραύνῳ
> πίονα μηρία κῆ' οὐδ' ἐξαίτους ἑκατόμβας,
> ὅσσα σὺ τῷ ἐδίδους.

(For no mortal ever burned as many rich thighpieces or choice hecatombs as you did in offerings to Zeus whose joy is in lightning.)

We may add another, less obvious parallel, one that, but for the foregoing considerations, might have carried comparatively little significance. In the narrative of Odysseus's life, Athena and Eurycleia serve functionally similar roles, different in degree perhaps, but not in kind. What Athena is to the mature Odysseus, Eurycleia was to the child. The nurturant concern for his well-being she showed when he was a child lives on unabated, for to her he will always be *teknon*. Her expression of concern for him—ὤ μοι ἐγὼ σέο, τέκνον, ἀμήχανος (363)—thematically echoes Athena's in 1.48: ἀλλά μοι ἀμφ᾽ Ὀδυσῆϊ δαΐφρονι δαίεται ἦτορ. In speeches of nearly identical length, Athena in book 1 and Eurycleia in book 19 touch on four common themes:

1. nurturant concern for Odysseus's welfare;
2. Zeus's anger as the cause of his suffering;
3. his piety as expressed in his sacrifices;
4. his ill treatment at female hands.

In short, then, the narrative frame is programming us to focus the same kind of attention on the significance of Odysseus's name in relationship to his fate as was required of us in book 1, except that here it occurs even before we have any inkling that the very story of the naming is about to be sprung on us with unusual abruptness and then told at such leisurely length that it has, as we observed, been narrowly judged ruinous to the dramatic effect of the narrative that frames it.

Irene J. F. De Jong argues persuasively that the story of Odysseus's scar represents a mental flashback of Eurycleia, "one of the rare long passages," she says, "where the point of view of a character is represented in the narrative instead of being expressed directly by the character in the form of a speech." If, as I have suggested, we take the story of Odysseus's naming as the focus of attention, there is good reason why the story should be told from Eurycleia's point of view, and why she should be the first person in Ithaca to recognize Odysseus. (Telemachus, remember, does not actually recognize Odysseus, but must take his identity on faith.) Eurycleia is the one human being best qualified to know not only what the name Odysseus refers to—its identifying description, but its sense as well.

First, the identifying description. It is Eurycleia who, as his nurse, spent more time with Odysseus than any other person in his life, a fact to which our attention is twice sharply drawn in this very passage, by Penelope just before the framed story of the naming and by Odysseus just after it. First, Penelope describes the maidservant who is going to bathe Odysseus's feet with these words: "I have a very shrewd-witted old woman who nursed that unfortunate man aright and raised him, taking him in her own hands the moment his mother bore him" (353–55). Then, immediately after the recognition, Odysseus says to Eurycleia, "It was you who nursed me at your very own breast" (482–83), and further warns her of the consequences if she breaks silence: "Nurse though you were to me, I shall not spare you" (489). As for the sense of his name, it was she—not his mother Anticleia, not his father Laertes—who offered the infant to his grandfather Autolycus for naming, and even, as we shall see, tactfully hinted what the name should be.

The main focus of our attention is this story of the naming. We shall return later to its narrative enclosure, the story of the scar, for the light it sheds on what it frames. To a reader prepared to disregard our observations on the role and words of Eurycleia, the first question that must arise is "What is this story of Odysseus's name doing here?" That is a reasonable question, for, from the point of view of its motivation, it seems quite superfluous. The run of the narrative, paraphrased to emphasize the thinness of its motivation, goes like this: Eurycleia recognizes the scar, which Odysseus got from a boar on Parnassus when he was visiting his maternal grandfather Autolycus, master among all men at thievery and equivocal oaths, the gifts of an eagerly sympathetic Hermes; on a trip to Ithaca once to visit his daughter and her newborn child, Autolycus had given Odysseus his name at Eurycleia's urging, and had promised to give him rich gifts when, on reaching puberty, the young man should pay his grandfather a visit; and that's what the young Odysseus was doing at Parnassus. So the tale of the scar, itself a "digression," is barely two lines under way when we are launched into the story of the naming, purportedly to explain why Odysseus had gone to visit Autolycus. Now that a grandson should be visiting his grandfather hardly seems like the kind of thing that needs an explanation, even less, so elaborate an explanation. As I have been arguing, unnecessary or flimsy motivation, here as elsewhere, should focus our attention all the more on function.

It is Eurycleia who takes what seems, for a slave, even as highly honored a slave as she is (1.432), a rather bold initiative in urging Autolycus to name the infant. That it should not be the child's father or mother who does this is curious enough. But there is another oddity. Although the narrator tells us that Autolycus responded to *her* (τὴν), his quoted words are directed to *Laertes and Anticleia* (405–6):

τὴν [sc. Εὐρυκλείαν] δ' αὖτ' Αὐτόλυκος ἀπαμείβετο
φώνησέν τε·
γαμβρὸς ἐμὸς θύγατέρ τε, τίθεσθ' ὄνομ' ὅττι κεν εἴπω.

I know of no usage of (ἀπ-)ἀμείβομαι that quite matches these conditions. It might suggest the deliberate alteration of an inherited tale in which not Eurycleia but Laertes or, perhaps better, Anticleia prompted Autolycus to name Odysseus, for her name is after all the metrical equivalent of Eurycleia's.[3]

But by far the most interesting feature of this passage,

---

[3] That Ἀντίκλεια was in fact the original reading here (401) is argued by Schwartz (1924: 116) and by Ameis and Hentze (1908–20: *ad* 19.401 and 406), and at least one manuscript cites it as a *varia lectio*.

and perhaps the point where our entire discussion of Odysseus's name reaches its sharpest and most significant focus, are two short speeches: one given to Eurycleia as she sets the infant on Autolycus's lap to be named; the other, already referred to in part, given to Autolycus as he responds to her. For not since Athena's pun in book 1 or the verbal pyrotechnics of the *outis* ploy in book 9 are we encouraged so explicitly to reflect on the referential and significant character of words (403–9):

Αὐτόλυκ᾽, αὐτὸς νῦν ὄνομ᾽ εὕρεο, ὅττι κε θεῖο
παιδὸς παιδὶ φίλῳ· πολυάρητος δέ τοί ἐστι.
τήν δ᾽ αὖτ᾽ Αὐτόλυκος ἀπαμείβετο φώνησέν τε·
γαμβρὸς ἐμὸς θύγατέρ τε, τίθεσθ᾽ ὄνομ᾽ ὅττι κεν εἴπω·
πολλοῖσιν γὰρ ἐγώ γε ὀδυσσάμενος τόδ᾽ ἱκάνω,
ἀνδράσιν ἠδὲ γυναιξὶν ἀνὰ χθόνα πουλυβότειραν·
τῷ δ᾽ Ὀδυσεὺς ὄνομ᾽ ἔστω ἐπώνυμον.

("Now, Autolycus, you yourself [*autos*] devise the name to give your own child's child. For he is *polyarētos*." To her Autolycus in turn responded with these words: "My son-in-law and daughter, call him by the name I say. My life to this point[4] has been marked by the hatred [*odyssamenos*] of many people, both men and women, all over the bountiful earth. So let his given name be Odysseus [Hate].")

We shall return to the meaning of πολυάρητος, which I have not translated above, later in our discussion. For the present, the first point to be made is that, in addressing Autolycus, Eurycleia is made to set the stage for Odysseus's significant naming by a play upon *Autolycus's* name: *Auto-lyk,' autos*, "You your*self, Self*-wolf,[5] devise the name. . . ."

---

[4] Some critics insist on taking τόδ᾽ ἱκάνω in the spatial sense ("I have reached this *place*," i.e., Ithaca). But ἱκάνω and ἱκνέομαι are frequently used in a temporal sense, as in such phrases as ἥβην or ἥβης μέτρον ἱ. (15.366, 18.217); ἐπί γηρᾶς or γήραος οὐδὸν ἱ. (8.227, 15.256); ἠῶ ἱ. (17.497); με παλαίφατα θέσφαθ᾽ ἱ. (9.507); τέλος ἵκεο μύθων (*Il.* 9.56); etc.

[5] Note that, for scientific etymology, the relationship between the two elements of Autolycus's name is not clear, and a few scholars hold that

We are invited to inspect the name of Autolycus for significance, especially in light of what has just been said of him by the narrative voice, and what he is shortly to say of himself. Autolycus is the unsocialized individualist (*autos*) par excellence, living wolf-like on the fringes of society, a cunning predator. His greatest skills, thievery and equivocation, gifts of Hermes, are perversions of the two essential bonds of social existence, exchange of material goods and the oath of trust. If we consider another fundamental feature of human social existence, the constraints associated with the exchange of women, then another story told of him, though not in Homer, fits the pattern of a life lived with little concern for the norms of the group: he was said to have secretly sent Anticleia to the bed of his houseguest Sisyphus, despite her betrothal to Laertes. What is more, he does not belong to a *dēmos*, nor does he dwell in a *polis* or an *astu*, but somewhere on the rugged slopes of Mount Parnassus, and a narrative otherwise obsessed with genealogy is curiously silent about his lineage, even in this passage where Hermes is declared to be his benefactor and avid supporter, but there is no mention that Hermes is his father, as in a Hesiodic fragment (64). There is, then, a measure of irony in this picture of the outlaw engaged in the essentially social act of naming, and in that very act declaring his own hostile distance from the human community.

The angry hatred that exists between Autolycus and society, then, becomes the source of Odysseus's name. In this there is much to concern ourselves with, but let us start with a question that has exercised philologists since the time of the Alexandrians. Who is the subject and who the object of the hatred expressed in the word ὀδυσσάμενος in 407? In other words, what is the grammatical voice of this participle? My own translation above ("My life . . . has been marked by the hatred of many people") is deliber-

---

the last element should be derived from *λύκη 'light', not λύκος 'wolf'. See *LfgrE* s.v. Αὐτόλυκος.

ately equivocal to reflect this problem. Is ὀδυσσάμενος passive, "hated," as interpreted by the scholiasts and most scholarship to the turn of the twentieth century? Or is it active (i.e., middle deponent), "hater," as unequivocally in all its other extant uses in archaic epic (e.g., in Athena's pun in 1.62) and in the reading of most scholars since the editions of Monro and Ameis-Hentze? Is Autolycus the hated or the hater? Stanford (1952) believes that the change in interpretation resulted from a change in scholarly perspective from a primarily ethical way of viewing the *Odyssey* to a more scientifically linguistic one. The latter view, I would urge, might be more aptly characterized as *statistical*, in the sense that the meaning of a word derived from its usage in a selection of other contexts carries more weight than the one believed to be demanded by the local syntactic or semantic context. The ancients apparently had no problem considering ὀδύσασθαι either active or passive. Alexandrian scholars of course could treat ὀδυσσάμενος passively because it is a comfortable commonplace in Alexandrian poetry to use the aorist middle form with passive meaning (Schwyzer 1938: 1.757; Wackernagel 1916: 19). A scholiast on Athena's pun in 1.62 says that οἱ παλαιοί ("the ancients") used this word for προσκροῦσθαι, which itself means either "to offend" or "to take offense at." Sophocles (fr. 880N) seems to be influenced by this passage when he interprets the etymology passively even though he clearly uses the verb actively:

ὀρθῶς δ᾽ Ὀδυσσεύς εἰμ᾽ ἐπώνυμος κακοῖς
πολλοὶ γὰρ ὠδύσαντο δυσσεβεῖς ἐμοί.

(In the eyes of evil men I am truly what my name Odysseus means, for the impious in large numbers have *hated* me.)

In his paraphrase of ὀδυσσάμενος, Eustathius goes beyond the ancients in absolutely excluding the active meaning here: πολλοῖς μισηθεὶς καὶ δι᾽ ὄργης ἐλθὼν παθητικῶς, οὐ μήν κατ᾽ ἐνέργειαν. In 1878 Merry began to show discomfort with the long-prevailing reading of ὀδυσσάμενος as passive, and suggested that it had "a double sense, as incurring and dealing out wrath." The 1889 edition of Ameis-Hentze also considered it ambiguous: ". . . einer, der gegen viele Hass gefasst hat, viele hassend: daher Ὀδυσσεύς 'der Hasser.' " By 1901 both Ameis-Hentze and Monro pronounce it active, largely for want of any other recorded passive usage.[6]

Leonard Palmer (1963b: 145) cites evidence that seems to make the "statistical" case even stronger. He follows Schwyzer (1938: 1:757) in noting the large number of so-called older, nonsigmatic aorists (e.g., ἠχθόμην, ἐβλήμην, ἐκτάμην, ἐπιθόμην) whose middle forms are used passively; but when it comes to sigmatic aorists (including presumably ὀδυσσάμενος), he appears, unlike Schwyzer (who with his contemporaries was still interpreting ὀδυσσάμενος passively), to follow the more current statistical trend in refusing to admit a passive function for the middle voice.[7]

Is this truly a dilemma in which we are compelled to choose between the active and the passive, and not, as with Merry and the early Ameis-Hentze, have it both ways? Our

---

[6] But Stanford sees no "unambiguous interpretation" in Monro's pronouncement, for, in his words (1952: 210), "Monro gives no cross-reference here to his revealing note on ἀπεχθόμενος in Odyssey 16.114. There he observes that elsewhere this verb is 'generally passive' (in fact it is always so in Homer, except here), but that in this instance it applies to both sides of the quarrel. He continues 'so probably in 19.407 ὀδυσσάμενος which is generally "having been angered" . . ., is used in the more comprehensive sense of "having quarrelled." ' In other words despite his insistence that the participle cannot have a passive sense, Monro's final translation closely approximates to Merry's preference for 'a double sense, as incurring and dealing out wrath.' "

[7] He thus concludes that the nonthematic middles used passively must be "fossilized survivors" in Homeric Greek. The same statistical pressure forces the sigmatic κρινάσθων in 8.36 to be ruled active, governed by some vague, indefinite subject: κούρω δὲ δύω καὶ πεντήκοντα / κρινάσθων is thus translated not "Let fifty-two young men be chosen" but "Let them choose fifty two young men." And in Simonides fr. 22D ἐπέξαθ᾽ ὁ κριός, since rams don't card or shear their own or anyone else's wool, nothing will work to save the statistics but for the statisticians to alter the text.

own unreflective linguistic habits, as in this case to think of active and passive voice as the most fundamental pair that exhausts the category of voice, can create a procrustean perspective that leads to impoverished readings. Historically in Indo-European, the most fundamental opposition appears not to have been between active and passive, but between active and *middle*, with the passive occupying a secondary and derivative position.[8] This primitive binary opposition between active and middle in Indo-European is thus described by Palmer (1980: 292):

> The active verb was used to present an activity proceeding from a subject outwards; when the event took place within the subject or was reflected on the subject, the middle voice was used. . . . Inherent in the middle is the notion of the "passive," formal grammatical distinction of which developed gradually in Greek.

J.-P. Vernant draws some rich though not uncontroversial conclusions from this bald overview of the evidence in a comment on Benveniste's *Nom d'action et nom d'agent dans les langues indo-européennes*. When we look at the active and middle as they are represented in Benveniste's work, he says,

> we see two cases, one in which the action is ascribed to the agent like an attribute to a subject, and another in which the action envelopes the agent and the agent remains immersed in the action—that is the case of the middle voice. The psychological conclusion that Benveniste doesn't draw, because he is not a psychologist, is that in thought as expressed in Greek or ancient Indo-European there is no idea of the agent being the *source* of his action. Or, if I may translate that, as a historian of Greek civilization, there is no category of the *will* in Greece.[9]

[8] Benveniste 1966; Chantraine 1963: 179–80; Lehmann 1974: 151, 183–84, who attributes the absence of a true passive to the absence of causative constructions in proto-Indo-European.

[9] From the discussion on Roland Barthes's paper "To Write: Intransi-

THE UNHALLOWED NAME OF ODYSSEUS   133

The original condition of the Greek language, even in the future and aorist (where later Greek morphologically distinguishes middle and passive), was one in which the middle forms had both middle and passive meanings, exclusively passive constructions being a later creation (Kühner, Blass, and Gerth 1890–1904: 2.114). In fact, even then, in archaic epic only about a quarter of the so-called aorist passives in -θην are purely passive (see above, pp. 115–16, Chantraine 1958: 399ff., 1963: 181; and Palmer 1980: 302). So what we find in Homer is a situation more closely approximating the condition of proto-Indo-European than that of later Greek and in the Western world generally, in which the middle voice loses ground to the passive and all but disappears. The concomitant cultural results of this development are summarized by Vernant: "What we see, . . . through language, the evolution of law, the creation of a vocabulary of the will, is precisely the idea of the human subject as agent, the source of actions, creating them, assuming them, carrying responsibility for them" (in Mackey and Donato 1970: 152). Parenthentically, one is tempted to see in this linguistic situation a parallel to the ambivalent attitude toward human action expressed, almost as if it were a programmatic statement, in Zeus's remarks, early in book 1 of the *Odyssey*, about the contending explanations of human suffering. Are mortals fully developed agents who must be held responsible for their actions, or are they for the most part passive objects of divine activity, or, what may be closer to the tonalities of the whole text when all its contending voices are averaged out, do they feel themselves immersed in the action in such a way that, at least at times, "doer" and "done to" become inadequate categories, drawing a sharp line, legislating a boundary, where none is felt?

What we have been saying about the early state of the

tive Verb?" in Macksey and Donato 1970: 152. See also his "Catégories de l'agent et de l'action en Grèce ancienne," in *Langue, discours, société: Pour E. Benveniste* (Paris, 1975), 365–73.

middle voice is especially true of so-called *verba affectuum*, verbs expressing emotion, such as *ὀδύσσομαι*. Such verbs normally appear in the middle voice and do not always make it clear whether the activity associated with the emotion is emanating from the subject of the sentence or directed toward it, or whether there is reciprocity in a plurality of emotionally implicated individuals (Schwyzer 1938: 2.228–29, 232, 236–37; Stanford 1952: 212). Our way of understanding or at least of expressing emotion— as something emanating from a subject toward an object, like a missile thrown by someone at someone else, or as something exchanged between two parties—is essentially itself highly metaphoric, and may blind us to a way of experiencing and expressing the emotion that concentrates on the activity as a kind of envelope embracing those involved with little apparent interest in distinguishing what we would call "agent" and "patient." Viewed in this way, "hatred" is an atmosphere in which the ὀδυσσάμενος finds himself immersed. Is Autolycus's exercise of his hermetic skills, *kleptosynē* and *horkos*, thievery and equivocation, the cause or the effect of the mutual antagonism between him and the normative community? And do we not have in the hatred of Autolycus the point where Bakhtin's two voices, centripetal and centrifugal, intersect?

Another point. That Autolycus should give his grandson so patently inauspicious a name has troubled many scholars. It has actually been urged against the Palmer/Nagy etymology of *Akhilleus* as "he who brings distress on the people" that "in real life no son would be given so inauspicious a name by his father" (Palmer 1980: 37). It is true that there is widespread belief, in ancient Greece and in many primitive societies, in the magical efficacy of the name and in its power to affect the destiny of its bearer, a belief that would naturally lead one to avoid inauspicious names. We should note parenthetically, however, that clear evidence for such a belief in Greek culture is relatively late; Homer shows no trace, at least no explicit trace, of it. But even beyond that, the objectors, in their view of what real life is, irrespective of the problematical relationship between literature and so-called "real life," are operating from a patently too narrow frame of cultural verisimilitude. The annals of anthropology show not a few cultures in which it is common for parents to give a name expressing their own state of mind or condition at or shortly before the child's birth, a name, in other words, which is meant to express the present or past of the namer, not the future of the named. What is more to our point, in some of these societies, as for example a Uganda tribe described by Claude Lévi-Strauss (1966: 179), most of these names are in fact uncomplimentary to one or both of the parents, even when *they* give the name. He cites such names as "In-laziness," given because the parents were slothful, "In-the-beer-pot," because the father was a drunkard, "Give-not," because the mother was niggardly in feeding the father. Lévi-Strauss (1966: 179–80) cites J.H.M. Beattie's discussion of a similar custom among the Banyoro. It is an explanation that closely parallels our analysis of the Autolycus passage in Homer. Such personal names

> "are concerned with the themes of death, sorrow, poverty, neighbourly spite." But "the person giving the name is almost always thought of as being acted upon, not as acting; the victim of the envy and hatred of others." This moral passivity, which projects upon the child an image of the self created by others, finds expression on the linguistic plane: ". . . the two verbs *to lose* and *to forget* are used in Lunyoro with the thing forgotten as the subject, the forgetter as the object . . . The loser or forgetter does not act upon things, they act upon him.'[10]

We would be incautious indeed, if we thought of this as "evidence" for what is going on in the Autolycus passage. Even as "parallel" it would not carry much weight were it not that archaic Greek myth and epos itself offers a number of examples other than the one we are here consider-

[10] Compare Greek λανθάνειν.

ing (Sulzberger 1926: 385ff.). In two separate passages in
the *Iliad*, we are told that Astyanax was named for the
character of his father (6.402–4; 22.505–7):

τὸν ῥ᾽ Ἕκτωρ καλέεσκε Σκαμάνδριον, αὐτὰρ οἱ ἄλλοι
᾽Αστυάνακτ᾽· οἷος γὰρ ἐρύετο Ἴλιον Ἕκτωρ.

(Hector used to call him Scamandrius, but others called him
Astyanax, for Hector alone protected Ilion.)

νῦν δ᾽ ἂν πολλὰ πάθῃσι, φίλου ἀπὸ πατρὸς ἁμαρτών,
᾽Αστυάναξ, ὃν Τρῶες ἐπίκλησιν καλέουσιν·
οἷος γὰρ σφιν ἔρυσο πύλας καὶ τείχεα μακρά.

(Having lost his father, sufferings in great number wait for
Astyanax; that's what the Trojans call him, for you [Hector]
alone protected the gates and long walls.)

Pausanias (10.26.4) tells us that in the *Cypria* the son of
Achilles was named Pyrrus by Lycomedes, but Neoptolemus by Phoenix "because Achilles had gotten his start in
warfare while still young" (ὅτι ᾽Αχιλλεὺς ἔτι νέος πο-
λεμεῖν ἤρξατο). The name could also mean "recently
(νέον) gone to war." Other names that seem to have been
derived in the same way are Telemachus, Telegonus, and
Ptoliporthes (a common epithet of his father Odysseus),
Peisistratus (for his father Nestor's persuasive power), Eu-
rysaces (for his father Ajax's great shield), and Gorgo-
phone (for her father Perseus's great exploit).[11]

These names are derived from a condition or characteristic of a parent, but none of them suggest embarrassment
or sorrow (unless, for want of context, we infer it in the
case of Neoptolemus). But of this type also we have unmistakable examples. The son Menelaus has by a slave woman
is called Megapenthes, presumably for the father's grief
over the loss of Helen (*Od.* 4.11). A story was told in the
Cypria (fr. 20 = Schol. ad Lycophron 570) of a son of Di-
onysus called Staphilus (a name, it should be noted, which
refers to his father). He has a daughter, Rhoeo (named for

---

[11] See Sulzberger 1926 for other examples.

her grandfather?), who is made pregnant by Apollo. In a pattern reminiscent of Danae, her father sets her adrift in a chest that lands at Euboea, where she gives birth to a child called Anios after the pain she had suffered because of him: ὃν Ἄνιον ἐκάλεσε διὰ τὸ ἀνιαθῆναι αὐτὴν δι᾽ αὐτόν. In the *Homeric Hymn to Aphrodite* (198–99), the goddess tells Anchises that their child will be named Aeneas after the terrible humiliation (*ainon akhos*) she feels for having slept with a mortal:

τῷ δὲ καὶ Αἰνείας ὄνομ᾽ ἔσσεται οὕνεκα μ᾽ αἰνὸν
ἔσχεν ἄχος ἕνεκα βροτοῦ ἀνέρος ἔμπεσον εὐνῇ.

Similarly, Cleopatra, the wife of Meleager in the *Iliad*, was really called Alcyone by her parents, because of the halcyon-like cry her mother had uttered when raped by Apollo (9.561–64):

τήν [Κλεοπ.] τότ᾽ ἐν μεγάροισι πατὴρ καὶ πότνια μήτηρ
᾽Αλκυόνην καλέεσκον ἐπώνυμον, οὕνεκ᾽ ἄρ᾽ αὐτῆς
μήτηρ ἀλκυόνος πολυπενθέος οἶτον ἔχουσα
κλαῖεν ὅ μιν ἑκάεργος ἀνήρπασε φοῖβος ᾽Απόλλων.

It is worth noting, incidentally, that this passage and the Autolycus passage in the *Odyssey* are probably among the oldest legendary material in Homer. Phoenix himself says as much of the Meleager story (9.527–28):

μέμνημαι τόδε ἔργον ἐγὼ πάλαι, οὔτι νέον γε,
ὡς ἦν.

And the Autolycus passage contains a reference to healing wounds by incantation (ἐπαοιδῇ δ᾽ αἷμα κελαινὸν / ἔσχεθον, 9.457–58), an apparently primitive practice[12] wholly unlike the practice of medicine elsewhere in Homer (*Iliad* 4.210–19; 5.899–904; 11.828–48).[13]

[12] Compare Lévi-Strauss's essay, "The Effectiveness of Symbols" 1963: 181–201.
[13] Sulzberger (1926: 408–9) argues that, excluding the divine names, historically the oldest form of naming in Greek epos and myth is one

Should we not also think of Anticleia, Odysseus's mother, as having been named in the same fashion for the bad reputation her father's antisocial practices earned him? It is also plausible, as was suggested earlier, to think of Arete's name as belonging to this class, meaning "Accursed" rather than "Prayed for (or to)," especially inasmuch as the first mention of her name comes in a genealogical setting that centers on the sad fate of her father, dying young and without male issue (ἄκουρος), still a bridegroom in his house, presumably before Arete's birth.

This consideration leads us directly back to an interesting detail in the story that was our point of departure. When Eurycleia presents the infant Odysseus to Autolycus for naming, she tells him that the child is πολυάρητος. Now clearly what she means to say is that he is "much-prayed-for"; the same expression is used in the *Homeric Hymn to Demeter* by Metaneira of her newborn son when she says to Demeter (219–20),

παῖδα δέ μοι τρέφε τόνδε, τὸν ὀψίγονον καὶ ἄελπτον
ὤπασαν ἀθάνατοι, <u>πολυάρητος</u> δέ μοί ἐστιν.

(Nurse this child for me, him whom the gods sent me late and beyond my expectations; to me he is *polyarētos*.)[14]

That Eurycleia may even be tactfully prompting Autolycus in what name to choose, either *Polyaretus* or *Aretus*, has long been the view of some readers. And we should not pass on without noting that the child who was "much-prayed-for;' in the framed story is now the grown man "much-prayed-for" in the framing context. But, more to our purpose, *polyarētos* is ambiguous and can as easily mean "much-cursed"—a close synonym, in fact, for the very word, *odyssamenos*, which motivates the name Autolycus chooses! The root seems to mean simply "prayer," leav-

---

derived from an event in the life of a parent or parents that shortly preceded the birth of the child.

[14] Note the interesting semantic tension between ἄελπτον and πολυάρητος.

ing it to context to specify beneficent or maleficent intentions. Statistically in extant usage the noun ἀρή (Attic ἀρά), the verb ἀράομαι, and especially the adjective ἀρητός, together with their compounds, show a heavy predominance on the side of the meaning "curse." Autolycus is master craftsman in the manipulation of verbal ambiguity into expedient oaths (*horkos*). Therefore, he cannot but be sensitive to the essential polysemy, the duplicity of language, as his grandson will learn to be. In naming Odysseus, then, does he not take his cue from the ambiguity of *polyarētos*? As *odyssamenos*, he himself has been *polyarētos*, the object of many imprecations. That is the social response to hostility, the very opposite of *kleos*, which is society's reward to the man without blame (ἀμύμων), as Penelope remarks in what sounds like a snatch of gnomic wisdom in the frame narrative leading up to the foot-bath (19.329–34):

ὅς μὲν ἀπηνὴς αὐτὸς ἔῃ καὶ ἀπηνέα εἰδῇ,
τῷ δὲ καταρῶνται πάντες βροτοὶ ἄλγε' ὀπίσσω
ζωῷ, ἀτὰρ τεθνεῶτί γ' ἐφεψιόωνται ἅπαντες·
ὅς δ' ἂν ἀμύμων αὐτὸς ἔῃ καὶ ἀμύμονα εἰδῇ,
τοῦ μέν τε κλέος εὐρὺ διὰ ξεῖνοι φορέουσι
πάντας ἐπ' ἀνθρώπους, πολλοί τέ μιν ἐσθλὸν ἔειπον.

(He who is hostile and whose mind is full of hostility all men curse [*katarōntai*] with anguish while he lives, all men mock in death; but the blameless man whose thoughts are blameless, his wide-ranging reputation strangers carry to the whole world, and many there are who speak well of him.)

Furthermore, as a dweller on the fringes of society, Autolycus is in a position to see more clearly the full implications of naming. To be named is to be categorized, to be located in a conventional social matrix, and thus, insofar as language has power to help or harm, to become the potential focus of praise or blame, of blessing or curse. To be named is to be given a socio-spatial locus, and, in 'Homeric society,' encouraged to perpetuate it temporally with *kleos* by the pursuit of society's sanctioned excellences. It is also to become, therefore, a focus, a target for curses.

From the standpoint of the frame story, *polyarētos* recalls what the framed story of Odysseus's naming anticipates: the encounter with Polyphemus. There the hero had preserved himself by congenital Autolycan *mētis* ("cunning intelligence") in contriving a name, *Outis*, that was in fact no name. That saving negativity is at work even earlier, for when questioned about his identity, Odysseus responds not with a typical heroic genealogy but rather with an uncharacteristic, merely generic identification and focuses on someone else's *kleos* (9.259–65): they are Achaeans, he says, contingents (λαοί) of Agamemnon, "whose *kleos* is the greatest under heaven, so great is the town he wrecked (διέπερσε πόλιν) and the multitudes he killed." When later he does indulge in the heroic norm of self-disclosure, he makes himself the focus of the Cyclops's curse. Polyphemus repeats verbatim the words from Odysseus's boast in which he declares his name, his lineage, and his homeland, using, significantly, an epithet of himself, πτολιπόρ-θιος ("town-wrecker"), which specifies not that saving capacity for intelligent contrivance, signified by such epithets as πολύμητις or πολυμήχανος, that sets him apart from heroic society, but the mark of the very heroic urge to individuating *kleos* that motivates the boast itself.[15]

Odysseus's boast (9.502–5):

> Κύκλωψ, αἴ κέν τίς σε καταθνητῶν ἀνθρώπων
> ὀφθαλμοῦ εἴρηται ἀεικελίην ἀλαωτύν,
> φάσθαι Ὀδυσσῆα πτολιπόρθιον ἐξαλαῶσαι,
> υἱὸν Λάερτεω, Ἰθάκη ἔνι οἰκί' ἔχοντα.

[15] Odysseus's loss through his insistence on naming himself has its counterpart in Polyphemus's loss through his insistence on naming his enemy. He loses the assistance of the other Cyclopes precisely because he uses the specific name "Outis" where an indefinite (such as τις or τινες) or even one of Odysseus's own less definite designations (Ἀχαιοί or λαοὶ Ἀτρεΐδεω Ἀγαμέμνονος) would have served his needs. Polyphemus, his savagery and solitude notwithstanding, is as preoccupied with the ideology of the person as any Iliadic hero.

(Cyclops, if anyone ever queries the outrage on your eye, tell him who blinded you, *Odysseus the town-wrecker, son of Laertes, who has his home in Ithaca.*)

Polyphemus's curse (9.528–31):

κλῦθι, Ποσείδαον γαιήοχε κυανοχαῖτα·
εἰ ἐτεόν γε σός εἰμι, πατὴρ δ' ἐμὸς εὔχεαι εἶναι,
δὸς μὴ 'Οδυσσῆα πτολιπόρθιον οἴκαδε ἱκέσθαι,
υἱὸν Λάερτεω, 'Ιθάκῃ ἔνι οἰκί' ἔχοντα.

Hear me, Poseidon, blue-girt earthshaker: if truly I am your son as is your claim, grant me that *Odysseus the town-wrecker, son of Laertes, who keeps his home in Ithaca*, never make it home.)

For the blinded Cyclops to hurl a missile in the direction of the hero's voice is a narrative parallel, a spatial metaphor for the social relationship between the curse and the name. When later, after a long delay, Odysseus finally discloses himself to the Phaeacians, it will not be the glory of the *ptoliporthios* that he boasts of, but his distinction in Autolycan deceit as if, both here (9.19–20) and in the ensuing self-narrative, to correct the imperfect identifying description of his name they have formed from the lays of Demodocus:[16]

εἴμ' 'Οδυσεὺς Λαερτιάδης, ὃς πᾶσι δόλοισιν
ἀνθρώποισι μέλω, καί μευ κλέος οὐρανὸν ἵκει.

(I am Odysseus, Laertes' son; my cunning wiles (*doloisin*) keep me on all men's mind. My reputation for them reaches heavenward.)

That way of expressing the cause of his fame (*kleos*) is interesting, for neither ancient nor modern critics are agreed on a univocal meaning for *pasi doloisin anthrōpoisi melō*. It can as easily mean "I am preeminent among men for cunning wiles" as "my cunning wiles make me a cause

---

[16] Cf. esp. 8.514, 516: ἤειδεν δ' ὡς ἄστυ διέπραθον. . . . ἄλλον δ' ἄλλῃ ἄειδε πόλιν κεραϊζέμεν.

of concern to men." (Even the syntax of *pasi* is a matter of choice: does it modify *doloisin* or *anthrōpoisi?*) In short, in the very act of formally identifying himself by name and patronymic, and of correcting the imperfect identifying description the Phaeacians have of him, he uses words containing an ambiguity closely analogous to the one we have observed in *polyarētos* and in *odyssamenos*.

It will be noticed that we have bypassed the story of the boar hunt on Parnassus to concentrate on the story that it in turn frames, how and why Autolycus gave Odysseus that particular name. In the next chapter, we return to the boar-hunt tale for the further light it sheds on the story of the naming, as well as on the story of how Odysseus unnames himself with *Outis*.

Chapter 6

OUTIS: THE NOMAN-CLATURE OF THE SELF

If "I"—true subject, subject of the unconscious—am
what I can be, "I" am always on the run. It is
precisely this open, unpredictable, piercing part of
the subject, this *infinite* potential to rise up, that the
"concept" of "character" excludes in advance.
—Hélène Cixous, "The Character of 'Character' "

Etant une personne, l'agent n'est personne.
—Claude Bremond, *Logique du récit*

FOR THE Greekless reader, a few words of explanation
about the title of this chapter are necessary. In Greek, the
word *ou* is the negative of fact and statement, while the
word *mē* is the negative of will and thought. Generally
speaking, *ou* is used with the indicative mood (for fact),
while *mē* is used with nonfactual moods, such as the sub-
junctive and optative. The word *tis* is an indefinite pronoun or adjective. Thus *ou tis* would mean "no one at all,"
or "no one in particular": "no man," the name, as we are
going to see, that Odysseus gives himself in the cave of the
Cyclops Polyphemus. The combination *mē tis* would mean
the same thing in a sentence with a nonfactual mood. But
looking just like this combination is a single word *mētis*, a
noun meaning cunning intelligence, and forming the second part of that frequently used epithet of Odysseus to
which we have often referred, *polymētis*, "(the person) of
much cunning intelligence." More of the elaborate pun on
that word in its place.

In the last chapter, we looked at the multiple narrative

frames in book 19: how Eurycleia's recognition frames the story of the boar hunt, which in its turn frames the story of how Odysseus's name was derived from the condition of Autolycus, later to become his own, as *polyarētos* and *odyssamenos*, a man much cursed, living in an exchange of mutual hostility. Before looking more closely at the story of the boar hunt, we should observe how even the names in the fictitious genealogy adopted by disguised Odysseus before his father (24.304–6) fall within the same semantic field as *polyarētos* and *odyssamenos*.

He calls himself Epēritos, son of Apheidas, and grandson of Polypēmōn, and says he comes from Alybas (εἰμὶ μὲν ἐξ Ἀλύβαντος . . . υἱὸς Ἀφείδαντος Πολυπημονίδαο . . . Ἐπήριτος). Both Epēritos, which looks like "man of *eris* (strife)," and Polypēmōn, the grandfather's name, which looks like "man of much woe," would be synonymous with *odyssamenos* and *polyarētos*. So also would Alybas, "land of distress (or struggle)" (ἀλύω), even if only by poetic or folk etymology, giving Epēritos, like Calypso, metaphoric geography to match the condition signified by his name. And Apheidas, "the unsparing," suggests the manner in which he has dealt with the suitors.[1] Wackernagel's "Chosen (or Picked) Man (= ἐπᾱριτος, cognate with ἀριθμός), son of Spare-nothing (in the monetary sense), and grandson of Much-wealth (= πολυπᾱμων, cf. *Il.* 4.433), from Silvertown" (ἐκ Σαλύβαντος, emended) better satisfies current state-of-the-art etymology and creates internal consistency among the four names, but in the process renders them arbitrary within the framework of the entire narrative.[2]

Polyarētos, Epēritos, Polypēmōn, Alybas: all are easy transformations of *odyssamenos*, the condition of mutual hostility. The action is active and/or passive, and in that it is analogous to the status of *polytropos*: the man of many

---

[1] Cf. 16.185 and esp. 22.54 for use of ἀφείδω in this sense.
[2] Wackernagel 1916: 249–51. On the concept of the "arbitrary," see above, Chapter 4, note 10.

turns is much turned against.[3] That is an apt note on which to return to the frame story of the boar hunt, just as the narrative itself resumes it after the centerpiece of the naming. We have observed how references to Eurycleia as nurse of Odysseus, coming at the points of transition from the outer narrative to the scar story and from the scar story back to the outer narrative, provide a kind of inexplicit "explanation" for the unusual role she plays in the story of Odysseus's naming. We have also suggested that Polyphemus hurling a boulder in the direction of Odysseus's voice is a more physical metaphor for, or (if you will) displays the same abstract narrative structure as, his curse in response to Odysseus's self-disclosure. Somewhat the same can be said of the framing tale of the boar hunt in relation to the story of the naming. Although it is motivated in such a way as to appear syntagmatically or metonymically related to the naming tale, in reality it recapitulates the latter by being a metaphoric substitute. The climax of the hunt is the collision of Odysseus and the boar, each pierced even as he pierces, a nearly simultaneous exchange of injuries that leaves the boar dead and Odysseus scarred for life (447–53):

> ὁ δ' ἄρα πρώτιστος 'Οδυσσεὺς
> ἔσσυτ' ἀνασχόμενος δολιχὸν δόρυ χειρὶ παχείῃ,
> οὐτάμεναι μεμαώς· ὁ δέ μιν φθάμενος ἔλασεν σῦς
> γουνὸς ὕπερ, πολλὸν δὲ διήφυσε σαρκὸς ὀδόντι
> λικριφὶς ἀΐξας, οὐδ' ὀστέον ἵκετο φωτός.
> τὸν δ' 'Οδυσεὺς οὔτησε τυχὼν κατὰ δεξιὸν ὦμον
> ἀντικρὺ δὲ διῆλθε φαεινοῦ δουρὸς ἀκωκή.

(Odysseus was the very first to charge, his powerful hand lifting the long spear for a fierce thrust. The boar caught him first, above the knee, his tusk gouging out flesh as he gored him aslant, but failed to strike bone. Odysseus had not

[3] One is reminded of an adage already considered ancient (τρίγερων μῦθος) in Aeschylus's day: δράσαντι παθεῖν (*Cho.* 313).

missed his shot, though, piercing the right shoulder, and the tip of the bright shaft went straight through.)

The word that triggered the double "digression" from the outer frame to the scar story to the naming story and that returns it to its point of departure in Penelope's chamber is οὐλή 'scar' (393, 464). A variant of the name of Odysseus, Οὐλίξης or Οὐλιξεύς, raises the same question posed in the case of Penelope. Is the similarity between the name and the action of the tale merely coincidental, or is there a causal connection, if not in Homer, where the variant names *Oulixes* and *Oulixeus* do not occur, then in some earlier or other narrative?[4] A more relevant question would be: To what extent does insisting on coincidence here impoverish the narrative? A richer alternative is to entertain the conjecture that we have two separate forms of the name of Odysseus, each recapitulating a separate narrative, one deriving the name from *oulē* 'scar,' and the other from **odysomai* 'hate,' both narratives brought together here, one encapsulating the other, but in such a way that they become metaphors for one another, for the hero's name itself, and for the blinding of Polyphemus followed by his retaliatory curse, all signifying the same thing: an exchange of injury.

The relationship between the boar hunt and the Cyclops episode bears closer scrutiny. To draw a connection, as we are about to do, between Odysseus's wounding thrust (οὐτάμεναι, οὐτήσε, 19.449, 352) in the boar hunt and the name *Outis*, which he calls himself in the Cyclops's cave, may seem boldly to cross the limits of verisimilitude, even for those sympathetic to the kind of reading here advocated, not to speak of those who espouse a more dogmatic philology. To account for the name *Outis*, it could be

---

[4] See Chantraine 1968–80 s.v. "Odysseus," for the possible confusion of pronounced λ with a δ-sound. Kretchmer suggests that the name with -δ- is relatively rare, outside of literary texts, in the oldest attested material. See also K. Marot (1960), who calls the Autolycus episode "ein heroisch zurechtgelegtes Erzählungszauberleid."

argued, it is sufficient to cite its homonymic relationship
with οὖτις 'no one,' which sets up the notorious failure in
communication when the wounded Polyphemus cries out
to the other Cyclopes. It is true that this is a sufficient explanation. But it is not an exhaustive one. The narrative
goes well beyond it, even at a quite explicit level, in establishing a connection between *Outis* and *mētis* ("cunning intelligence"), a connection that, strictly from the narrative
point of view, is unnecessary. By "unnecessary" here I
mean its relation to the narrative is not a metonymic (or
syntagmatic) one of implication, exclusion, compatibility,
or presupposition. It rather bears a metaphoric (or paradigmatic) relation to the whole incident, or at least to that
part of it which we might label the ruse of Odysseus.

The word *mētis*, meaning "cunning intelligence," recapitulates the incident the way a name presumes to recapitulate its identifying description, and it does it the way a *significant* name purports to do it, by finding (or forging) a
causal, syntagmatic connection between it and an element
within the narrative chain. There is an explosion of verbal
subtlety worthy of an Autolycus in the passage beginning
with the questions asked by Polyphemus's neighbors when
they are awakened by his outcries (9.405–14):

"ἦ μή τίς σευ μῆλα βροτῶν ἀέκοντος ἐλαύνει;
ἦ μή τίς σ᾽ αὐτὸν κτείνει δόλῳ ἠὲ βίηφι;"
τοὺς δ᾽ αὖτ᾽ ἐξ ἄντρου προσέφη κρατερὸς Πολύφημος·
"ὦ φίλοι, Οὖτίς με κτείνει δόλῳ οὐδὲ βίηφιν."
οἱ δ᾽ ἀπαμειβόμενοι ἔπεα πτερόεντ᾽ ἀγόρευον·
"εἰ μὲν δὴ μή τίς σε βιάζεται οἶον ἐόντα,
νοῦσον γ᾽ οὔ πως ἔστι Διὸς μεγάλου ἀλέασθαι,
ἀλλὰ σύ γ᾽ εὔχεο πατρὶ Ποσειδάωνι ἄνακτι."
ὣς ἄρ᾽ ἔφαν ἀπιόντες, ἐμὸν δ᾽ ἐγέλασσε φίλον κῆρ,
ὡς ὄνομ᾽ ἐξαπάτησαν ἐμὸν καί μῆτις ἀμύμων.

("Surely no one [*mē tis*] of mortal men is driving off your
flocks against your will? As for yourself, surely no one [*mē tis*]
is killing you by fraud or force?"

From within the cave, strong Polyphemus answered them: "Noman [*Outis*] is killing me by fraud and not by force."

In response they addressed him with winged words: "Well, if no man [*mē tis*] is using force on you, alone as you are, then surely there's no escaping the illness sent by great Zeus. For your part, you'd better pray to lord Poseidon, your father."

These were their words as they left, but the heart within me laughed at the way my name [*onoma*] and flawless cunning [*mētis*] had worked their deception.)

The verbal pyrotechnics here have long been appreciated:[5] the way in which the Cyclopes begin two questions with *ē mē tis*, "Surely no one . . ."; the joy Odysseus takes in

---

[5] Two of the more interesting among recent readings are Austin 1972 and Bergren 1983. On *mētis* in general, see especially Pucci 1986, and Detienne and Vernant 1978, esp. ch. 4. I quote at length their discussion of the differences in archaic Greek thought between Themis and Metis because it reads like a mythological version of Bakhtin's "centripetal" and "centrifugal" voices and represents yet another way the polarity between myth and *Märchen* that is one of the chief presuppositions of our approach in this study (107–8): "The omniscience of Themis relates to an order conceived as already inaugurated and henceforth definitively fixed and stable. Her pronouncements have the force of assertoric or categorical propositions. She spells out the future as if it was already written and since she expresses what will be as if it were what is, she gives no advice but rather pronounces sentence; she commands or she forbids. Metis, by contrast, relates to the future seen from the point of view of its uncertainties: her pronouncements are hypothetical or problematical statements. She advises what should be done so that things may turn out one way rather than another; she tells of the future not as something already fixed but as holding possible good or evil fortunes and her crafty knowledge reveals the means of making things turn out for the better rather than for the worse. Themis represents the aspects of stability, continuity and regularity in the world of the gods: the permanence of order, the cyclical return of the seasons (she is the mother of the *Hōrai*), the fixity of destiny (she is also the mother of the *Moirai* who 'give either good fortune or bad to mortal men'). Her role is to indicate what is forbidden, what frontiers must not be crossed and the hierarchy that must be respected for each individual to be kept forever within the limits of his own domain and status. Metis, on the other hand, intervenes at moments when the divine world seems to be still in movement or when the balance of the powers which operate within it appears to be momentarily upset."

his *onoma* ("name," i.e., *Outis*) and his *mētis* ("cleverness"), linking them together as one; the even subtler way in which Polyphemus's words Οὖτίς με κτείνει δόλῳ οὐδὲ βίηφιν, by which he means "Outis is killing me by fraud *and not* by force," is misunderstood by the other Cyclopes to mean "No one is killing me *either* by fraud *or* by force"; and finally the closing statement of Polyphemus's neighbors, "If *mētis* is using force on you," etc., which identifies Odysseus with cunning intelligence, and cunning intelligence with the abandonment of the *proper*, with the renunciation of what is personally distinctive. And the deliberateness with which this identification is being pressed is further underscored by the fact that in the expression εἰ μή τίς σε βιάζεται, "If *mētis* is using force on you," we have the only known exception to the rule requiring *ou* (not *mē*) in subordinate clauses with the indicative that precede the principal clause (Chantraine 1963: 333; Shipp 1972: 145; Heubeck 1986: *ad loc.*). Furthermore, the same expression plays openly with the contrast between *mētis* ("cunning intelligence") and *bia* ("force") already posed in the Cyclopes's question and in Polyphemus's response: δόλῳ οὐδὲ βίηφιν. Enforced sensitivity to the play of linguistic ambiguity is more intense nowhere in the poem.

It is in just such a charged linguistic environment that the hypothetical relationship between the name Outis and the verb οὐτάω 'pierce' is being proposed. This is, after all, a story about the *piercing* of the Cyclops's eye. Now the verb οὐτάειν 'to pierce' is not used in the description of the blinding, though it had been used a bit earlier, at the point where Odysseus had contemplated killing Polyphemus in his sleep (299–301):

τὸν μὲν ἐγώ βούλευσα . . .

. . . .

οὐτάμεναι πρὸς στῆθος, ὅθι φρένες ἧπαρ ἔχουσι.

(I wanted to *pierce* him in the chest, just where the midriff holds the liver.)

Is the relationship therefore to be ruled out because it is not displayed on the surface of the text, like the play on *Outis* and *mētis*? On the same grounds we would have to reject the relationships we have seen between Eumaeus's name and his function, and between Penelope's name and the story of her weaving, for in neither case does the verbal root find its way explicitly into the text. Is it merely a negligible coincidence that, in a story about the piercing out of an eye, a name (Οὖτις) explicitly motivated by its resemblance to the word for "no one" (οὖτις) also resembles, in the way that folk etymologies work, the word for "pierce" (οὐτάω)? To say "Yes, it fits, but it's only a coincidence" is to invoke the notion of an authoritative reading, to dogmatize about which likenesses are "acceptable" and which are not, to police the free play of metaphor, in a text less likely than we modern readers are to tolerate, if even to comprehend, the very notion of "mere coincidence" or the accidental. Which perspective is more likely to open up a text, the traditional philologist's deep suspicion of "unconscious meaning," or the principle expressed by Roman Jakobson, the tireless investigator of just such subliminal linguistic events: that the so-called accidental may be an instance of a yet-undiscovered rule (Jakobson 1978, 1985, and 1987: 250–61)?

Let us press the issue further. Once the homonymic relationship between οὐτάω and Οὖτις is registered, it may initiate a perspective for seeing the boar-hunt passage and the Cyclops episode as doublets on a larger scale. I am not speaking here of the obvious fact that in both passages there is an intense preoccupation with naming. That is significant enough. I am speaking rather of an abstract narrative structure on which both episodes could be modelled without sacrificing much in the way of significant detail.

To begin with, in both passages the aggressive character of Odysseus is highlighted. In the Cyclops's cave, after provisioning himself, Odysseus refuses the entreaties of his men to return to the ship, and after the blinding twice insults his victim despite the danger, leading to the disclosure of his name and the retaliatory curse that earns Odysseus another ten years of wandering. In the hunt on Parnassus, he is the very first, *prōtistos* (19.447), in the assault on the boar. Second, both passages emphasize the uncivilized, wild remoteness of the locale. The Cyclopes as a group live in caves far from other men, ignorant of agriculture, building crafts, cooking, and community assemblies, and from them Polyphemus dwells in even remoter solitude (οἶος . . . ἀπόπροθεν· οὐδὲ μετ' ἄλλους / πωλεῖτ', ἀλλ' ἀπάνευθεν ἐὼν . . . , 9.188–89). In book 19, the boar's lair lies in a thick wood on Mount Parnassus, and is so densely covered with leaves that no wind, rain, or sunlight penetrates it (439–43). Third, Odysseus survives to report the story skillfully and in detail. The Cyclops episode is part of Odysseus's own story, for which Alcinous commends his μορφὴ ἐπέων, the professional character of his storytelling (11.368):

μῦθον δ' ὡς ὅτ' ἀοιδὸς ἐπισταμένως κατέλεξας.

(You tell a tale with the same skill and orderly detail as a professional singer.)

A similar phrase—εὖ κατέλεξεν (19.464)—is used of the story of the boar hunt recounted by the young Odysseus to his parents. Both incidents, in short, display an identical pattern: an agent invades, penetrates a wild and remote natural environment undisturbed before his arrival, is confronted by one of its denizens, with whom he engages in a mutual exchange of injury, later to give a skillful account of it in detail.

This way of reading brings into conceptual interrelationship several ideas: (1) the piercing assault on the border of the other followed by retaliation and injury to the first attacker; (2) the social negativity of the name Outis, itself prepared for by the refusal of Odysseus to do any more than locate himself anonymously in his group in response to Polyphemus's first query about his identity, this all the more striking in a heroic context where self-disclosure is highly valued, and underscored through narrative analysis by the thinness of its motivation (see above, p. 46); (3) the paradoxical character of *mētis*, at once negative, withdrawn, secret, hidden, even playful (ἐμὸν δ᾽ ἐγέλασσε φίλον κῆρ, 9.413) on the one side, and on the other capable of inflicting great harm;[6] (4) the two-sidedness of Odyssean intelligence, looking before and after, as capable of assertive, preemptive action as of narrative reflection on it. In this context the autonomous power of the self, as well as its safety from peril, is associated not with the name and its heroic assertion, but with its denial or absence, with anonymity, in effect.

But a more crucial point, perhaps, is implicit in the use of Outis. Far from establishing and declaring the individuality of the self, paradoxically names merely classify, endow the named with group identification, but not with authentic individuation. What narrative does to the intractable flux of unprocessed sensations and memories, naming does more radically to narrative. In each case a powerful process of abstraction and stabilization works to immobilize and simplify the world of change. Naming is the extreme form of categorization because it takes what most philosophers have thought to be incomprehensible—the *individuum*—and creates the illusion that it has been trapped in comprehension.

This situation is exacerbated under the ideology of *kleos*, which motivates the Iliadic hero. Here the name, instead of referring as it presumes to do to the totality of the person named, is constrained to a narrowed focus on a single predicate, and indeed is turned, along with its designee, into what is presumed to be a socially beneficial paradigm, the semantic equivalent of that predicate: e.g., Achilles becomes the paradigm of courage, Nestor of persuasive wisdom, Penelope of feminine fidelity, etc. The true individual is nameless, or withholds his name; he is Outis. The Homeric poems represent a heroic culture that makes so-

---

[6] Note that in the vast majority of its archaic usages, the goal of *mētis* is injury.

cial appellation (καλεῖσθαι) synonymous with existence (εἶναι; L. P. Rank 1951: 25), but that fails to recognize, as so many cultures do, that individuation escapes predication, and can only be signified by the negative judgment implicit in *Outis*. Philosophical reflection and anthropological evidence support this (see, e. g., Lévi-Strauss 1966: 172–216; Derrida 1976: 107–18). Individuality, by definition, is precisely the unclassifiable. It is the irreducible residue that remains when all generic, classificatory, categorizing predication has been exhausted. It is *sui generis*. As such it is unknowable, or at least its intelligibility is the focus of fierce philosophical debate involving the compatibility of sameness and change. In the context of narrative (and perhaps also of "real life"), there are those who, like Roland Barthes, link this residue to an "ideology of the person," which tries to mask the fact that what we call the person is no more than a collection of generic adjectives, attributes, predicates ("semes" Barthes calls them):

> What gives the illusion that the sum is supplemented by a precious remainder (something like *individuality*, in that, qualitative and ineffable, it may escape the vulgar bookkeeping of compositional characters) is the Proper Name, the difference completed by what is *proper* to it. The proper name enables the person to exist outside the semes [or predicates], whose sum nonetheless constitutes it entirely. As soon as the name exists (even a pronoun) to flow toward and fasten onto, the semes become predicates, inductors of truth, and the Name becomes a subject: we can say that what is proper to narrative is not action but the character as Proper Name: the semic raw material . . . *completes* what is proper to being, *fills* the name with adjectives. (Barthes 1974: 191)

This point is made more neatly by Todorov and Bremond. Here is Bremond (1973: 104) summarizing Todorov's discussion (1969: 27–28):

> The agent is a person; but this person (or the proper name which designates it) is in itself dispossessed of any stable property. Its descriptive character is reduced to a minimum.

As a person, the agent is no one [*Etant une personne, l'agent n'est personne*]: "it is rather like an empty form which the different predicates (verb or attribute) come to fill." Every agent can enter into unstable relationship with any predicate; he is, so to speak, married to no one [*il n'est marié avec aucun*].[7]

Barthes's "ideology of the person" turns out to be another name for what we have identified as the ideology of *kleos*.

Odysseus's abrogation of distinctness points to a powerful paradox in the name *Outis*. The proper name never means the same thing to different people; it will always carry a different identifying description. That is a subtlely concealed flaw in the ideology of *kleos*. But "Outis," by the very austerity of its semantic content, being the negation of the indefinite, has a far greater chance of achieving univocality. What is more, precisely because it means "no one," it is the term least likely to be chosen as a name, especially for a member of heroic society. So when it *is* in fact chosen, as in Odysseus's case, it becomes the only truly "singular proper name," for it is not, nor is it ever likely to be, shared by another. (In this respect, it is not unlike the names of the gods.) Paradoxically, distinction is achieved through the abrogation of distinctness.

From this point of view, at once austere and discomfiting, Outis becomes the only *proper* name for the emptiness that in reality all narrative persons share, but that is nonetheless the improper ground on which their spurious

---

[7] Those put off by the gallic acidity of these representations of character may find, perhaps, more intelligibility but certainly no more comfort in William Gass's expression of the same idea. In discussing a character in *The Awkward Age*, he asks (1970: 44), "What is Mr. Cashmore? Here is the answer I shall give: Mr. Cashmore is (1) a noise, (2) a proper name, (3) a complex system of ideas, (4) a controlling conception, (5) an instrument of verbal organization, (6) a pretended mode of referring, (7) a source of verbal energy. But Mr. Cashmore is not a person." And again, he writes (50): "Normally, characters are fictional human beings and thus are given proper names. In such cases, to create a character is to give meaning to an unknown X; it is *absolutely* to *define*; and since nothing in life corresponds to these X's, their reality is borne by their name. They *are*, where it *is*."

claims to absolute distinctness rest. Odysseus's deliberate abrogation of distinctness displays him as the narrative agent par excellence, as therefore capable of becoming *any* character, of assuming *any* predicate, of doing or enduring *anything*, of being, in a word, *polytropos*. In retrospect from book 9, the fuller implications of the proem's first line and suppressed name emerge. Outis is *polytropos*, the negativity capable of the fullest and most polymorphic narrative development. Thus, within the poem, Odysseus-Outis-polytropos becomes a metaphor for the fundamental operations out of which narrative is generated. This will manifest itself in a variety of concrete ways, as for example even on a purely verbal and formulaic level, by endowing Odysseus, among all male Homeric figures, with a virtual monopoly of epithets in πολυ- (see Stanford 1950: 108–10).

The conception of individuality—or should we say nonindividuality?—articulated here virtually eliminates that nagging conventional scandal we have been educated to feel in Penelope's reluctance to recognize Odysseus in book 23. It goes beyond the simple need to test this man in her turn, just as he had been compelled, quietly and slowly, in safe anonymity, to test whether this was the "same" Penelope he left twenty years before (see Pucci 1987: 93). His need to test and her reluctance to recognize him turn out to be more compatible with the philosophical and semiotic problem of individuation than with an unreflective, conventional notion of a permanent individuality, the underlying subject of attributes and actions, the stable referent of the proper name. The compatibility of sameness and change is a greater problem for Penelope than for readers of her story with a heavy investment in the ideology of personal identity, who may also have been tricked into ignoring the difference between the duration of events and that of their narration, or, in other words, the difference between a twenty-year separation and the amount of time it takes to tell the story of a twenty-year separation. Penelope's situation is not only emotionally and psychologically traumatic, but philosophically interesting. What enables her to say, in spite of the changes wrought by twenty years' time, that the person who calls himself Odysseus, before her now, is the person called Odysseus whom she knew when he sailed from Ithaca? And even if he is the "same" person, in what *tropos* has *polytropos* returned? As *ptoliporthios* 'town-wrecker,' fresh from the slaughter of the suitors, in the one guise, now so prominent, that she is least likely to have known before? No Penelope welcomes the same Odysseus twice. Her syntax (23.175–76), showing the linguistic strain of the problem, has been attributed variously to "confused abridgement" of a more accurate expression (Stanford 1965 *ad loc.*) or to "feminine syntax" (meaning "emotional," "confused," "irregular"!).[8] Accordingly, it has tested the outer limits of the translator's skill. The sense requires something like "I know that *he* was the way *you* now appear when he left for Troy," but what comes out is something that defies easy translation. Fitzgerald manages it as well as can be hoped for: "I know so well how you—how he—appeared / boarding the ship for Troy."

μάλα δ᾽ εὖ οἶδ᾽ οἷος ἔησθα
ἐξ ᾽Ιθάκης ἐπὶ νηὸς ἰὼν δολιχηρέτμοιο.

Philosophers cite two competing criteria for the reidentification of persons: the identity of the bodies that they have or the identity of their sets of memories. Whatever view one may espouse in this debate, it is interesting that Penelope applies *both* criteria. She does not, as Eurycleia had done, simply settle for the scar, which for the nurse is a *sēma ariphrades* (an "unequivocal sign," 23.73), but which for her is a difficult (94–95), merely bodily recognition. Though she appears finally to admit to this bodily recognition in the passage just cited, she nonetheless presses for the *sēmata kekrymmena* (the "unapparent signs," 110), the

---

[8] B. L. Gildersleeve in his review of M. Bréal, *Pour mieux connaître Homère*, *American Journal of Philology* 28 (1907): 209.

memories shared alone with the person who left her twenty years before, the private memories of the immovable bed, the work of his own hands. Eurycleia had been the first to recognize Odysseus, for she knows him primarily under a superficial aspect that for her has not and could not change. For her, the nurse, he was and still is *teknon*, the object of potential help or harm. It is therefore appropriate that she should recognize him by the superficial *sēma* of the scar, the mark of an assault upon his young body, a public token of his suffering. By contrast, Penelope, the wife, is interested in the mutable subject, the changeable agent; for her the most convincing *sēmata* will be the hidden memories of himself as maker, the secret narrative of him that no one but she and he can tell. Until these *sēmata kekrymmena* (110) become *ariphradea* (225), until she is assured that the man before her is the "same" as the one who left her, the "same" character in the story she remembers of him, as unaltered as the immovable bed, her heart will not be persuaded (230).

For Penelope's ever-incredulous heart (θυμὸς . . . αἰὲν ἄπιστος 23.72), the visible, "unequivocal sign" (*sēma ariphrades*) is at best an unstable token, at worst an illusion. At this very moment, as she stands before the man with her husband's scar and her husband's name, she has good reason to cling desperately (but shrewdly) to her incredulity about the world. For even as they speak, the house resounds with sweet music and the din of dancing feet, deceptive contrivances of this Odysseus's *mētis* (125), but a clear sign, for all the world knows, that a wedding, not a bloodbath, has taken place. And throughout the neighborhood and in the streets, faithful Penelope's name is in public disgrace, subject of a tale till then merely possible, now actual, but false (148–51):

ὧδε δέ τις εἴπεσκε δόμων ἔκτοσθεν ἀκούων·
"ἦ μάλα δή τις ἔγημε πολυμνήστην βασίλειαν·
σχελίη, οὐδ' ἔτλη πόσιος οὗ κουριδίοιο
εἴρυσθαι μέγα δῶμα διαμπερές, εἷος ἵκοιτο."

(Anyone outside the house hearing [the music and dancing]
would say, "There you have it! Someone's married the queen
so many courted. The shameless bitch! She couldn't hold out
to keep her dear husband's estate until his return.")

What is more, the very words *sēma ariphrades* had been
used by Tiresias in his prophecy of the inland journey
(11.126), the account of which Odysseus is about to give
Penelope (23.265–84). There, paradoxically, the "unequivocal sign" is implicated in a realization of the sign's unstable relation with what it signifies. For not only will one object be mistaken for another—an oar for a winnowing-
fan—but the mistaken object will be given an exotic, unfamiliar name—ἀθηρηλοιγός for πτυόν—the alien speaker
thus indeliberately playing the poet's role, recategorizing
the world through metaphor, as the poet himself deliberately has done but three lines before, and with respect to
the same object, when he has Tiresias speak of oars as
"wings for ships to fly on" (ἐρετμά, τά τε πτερὰ νηυσὶ
πέλονται, 11.125 = 23.272). Parenthetically, it is no accident that in both cases, the new names shatter the opacity
of old, familiar nomenclature, and bring their objects'
functions, their actions in the world, freshly back to mind.

In the *Iliad*, it was the same, even if less articulate, realization of the sign's unstable condition and the precarious
relation between it and what it purports to signify that
brought Achilles' condition to crisis. Once his status is
seen to depend on so inconstant and abductable a token as
Briseis, once the link between trophy (*geras*) and the glory
it signifies is shown for the frangible thing it is, then he
must be made to wonder, as he appears to be doing in the
Embassy scene, how truly that status can be restored, and
for how long sustained, even by the splendid catalogue of
Agamemnon's propitiatory gifts. What abiding power to
signify can they possibly have? The "centripetal" epic voice
supporting the ideology of *kleos* is dominant enough in the
Iliad to keep this realization dim and to muddle its clear
expression, yet we are made to see that while the hero may
think he has escaped the vagaries of time and history by

leaving behind his imperishable fame (κλέος ἄφθιτον), that trace, that story, that sign or *sēma*, like any *sēma*, is as vulnerable as the hero's *geras* or his mortal body. This message quietly comes through during the funeral games for Patroclus in book 23. Nestor, in instructing his son Antilochus how to maneuver his horses in the tightest possible turn around the τέρμα, speaks of that turning point as follows (23.331–33):

> ἤ τευ σῆμα βροτοῖο πάλαι κατατεθνηῶτος,
> ἤ τό γε νύσσα τέτυκτο ἐπὶ προτέρων ἀνθρώπων,
> καὶ νῦν τέρματ᾽ ἔθηκε ποδάρκης δῖος Ἀχιλλεύς.

("It is either the tomb of some man who died a long time
    ago,
Or it was a racing-goal in the times of earlier men.
Now swift-footed brilliant Achilles has set it up as the
    turning-point.")

Gregory Nagy, in his study of this passage (1983), is right to point out the incontestable importance of the heroic σῆμα 'tomb' as a signifier of the absent signified, the dead hero, and that in this it is the visual counterpart of *epos*, another reminder of the absent hero's *kleos*. Unlike Nagy, however, I read a terrible irony in Nestor's remark, "either it is the *sēma* of some man who died a long time ago, or it was a racing-goal in the times of earlier men." For here is an object in the landscape that time's ravages have so divested of distinctive features that it has lost its "signified." Its hero, if it ever was a *sēma*, is anonymous. And, what is worse, even its character as *sēma*, as "signifier," is in doubt. So precarious and impermanent is the *kleos* it was meant, if it was a *sēma*, to preserve beyond its hero's death. In the context of this mute, unclear, and merely possible sign of heroic endeavor, are we meant to read ironically the ultimate fate of the Hellespontine *sēma* of Achilles and Patroclus, a *sēma* constructed so as "to shine clear a far way off," as we are told in *Odyssey* 24.83–84, "for men now living and those who will be hereafter"?

. . . ὥς κεν τηλεφανὴς ἐκ ποντόφιν ἀνδράσιν εἴη
τοῖσ᾽, οἳ νῦν γεγάασι καὶ οἳ μετόπισθεν ἔσονται.

In this *sēma* 'sign,' may we not understand the fate of all
heroic *sēmata* 'tombs'? The fate of all *sēmata* 'signs'? Erosion, deformation, transformation, reutilization, incessant
shifting from one code to another, possibly even utter
obliteration.[9]

Is it possible that, at least in part, this recognition of the
sign's instability, and the skill to exploit it, lies at the heart
of what is meant by *mētis*, shared with varying degrees of
self-consciousness by Penelope, Odysseus, Autolycus,
Achilles, Athena, the *Odyssey* poet himself? If that is so,
then, in the encounter with someone at least as well en-
dowed with that same recognition and skill, where the genuine limits of *mētis* are discovered, the need for mutual
trust also will be revealed. Perhaps nowhere does Odysseus
show himself less master of the situation, his *mētis* matched
and for the moment neutralized, than in his confrontation
with Penelope. In this scene he recognizes, amidst discom-
fiture and anger (ὀχθήσας, 23.182), that his olive-trunk
bedpost, however thick and deep-rooted in the earth, can
be undercut, displaced, and may have been. In that moment he faces the realization, as Achilles had, that the *sēma*
he thought to have made so stable is subject to change.
Whatever stability it is to have depends on Penelope. To
have undercut the firmly rooted trunk means to have un-
dermined the old bond these two shared, the bond of love
and trust. From this point of view, thematic reconciliation
is found for the philological quandary about the meaning
of *thesmon* in λέκτροιο παλαιοῦ θεσμὸν ἵκοντο ("they re-
tired to the *thesmon* [= *rite*? or *place*?] of their bed of old,"

---

[9] I first presented this observation in a paper entitled "Methodological
Rigor in *The Best of the Achaeans*" at a special panel during the annual
meeting of the American Philological Association in 1983. Since then a
similar point has been made by Lynn-George 1988: 265–66, who then
goes on admirably to spell out the vulnerability of both visual and textual
sēmata as vehicles of *kleos aphthiton*.

23.296), for their *bond* is in fact integrally linked if not identical to the *placement* of this bed.[10] We have suggested that Odysseus under the name of Outis represents the fundamental potentiality of the narrative "subject" to take on any attribute, to be linked with any action. It is therefore associated with *mētis*, that hidden power of cunning intelligence to find a way (*poros*) through the problematical,[11] and with *polytropos*, in its active sense the attribute to assume any attribute. We have here a paradoxical combination of negativity, withholding, and withdrawal on the one side, and individuality, power, and freedom on the other. Odysseus is never more himself, *autos*, than when he is *Outis*.

But that is only half the picture. For no man can be fully Outis; no man, as Alcinous says in a passage cited early in this investigation, is wholly without a name (8.552–54):

οὐ μὲν γάρ τις πάμπαν ἀνώνυμός ἐστ᾽ ἀνθρώπων,
οὐ κακὸς οὐδὲ μὲν ἐσθλός, ἐπὴν τὰ πρῶτα γένηται
ἀλλ᾽ ἐπὶ πᾶσι τίθενται, ἐπεί κε τέκωσι, τοκῆες.

(For wholly nameless is no man, be he wretch or nobleman, from the time of his birth, but parents lay names on everyone whenever they bring them into the world.)

Everyone is born into a social context, named, classified, located in society before one has any say in the matter, as a powerless, neuter *teknon*, object not subject, patient not agent. One is fixed within a system of constraints that both limits one's own power to act and makes one a clear focus or target for the activity of others. The name defines, sets limits, gives others control over the named, whether in the superstitious sense in which Polyphemus is able to curse Odysseus only after he gets his name or in the more general sense in which social expectations and restrictions

[10] On the meaning of θεσμόν here, see Russo 1985: 317 *ad* 23.296.
[11] Compare how in Plato's *Symposium* (203bff.) Mētis is the mother of Poros who is united with Penia to give birth to Eros. Cf. Detienne and Vernant 1978: 144.

arise out of the place one is given, the category assigned, by the name. Furthermore, the precise terms of this social classification are not given him to know with certainty, but must be accepted on faith. As Telemachus remarks on the question of his father's identity, "No man by himself ever gets clear knowledge of his own engendering," of how or when or where or by whom he was fathered (1.216):

οὐ γάρ πώ τις ἑὸν γόνον αὐτὸς ἀνέγνω.

The man who is *polytropos* cannot be pantropic, much less autotropic. Utterly to break free of social definitions and constraints is a humanly impossible dream,[12] which is expressed, as human impossibilities often are, in a "centrifugal" narrative of divine possibility, giving us in the *Homeric Hymn to Hermes* the story of the baby Hermes, consummate embodiment of *mētis*, who within hours of his birth and before anyone has given him a name, takes up the lyre, instrument of his own recent invention, and *improvises* (ἄειδε / ἐξ αὐτοσχεδίης, 54–55) a song of his own begetting with his name in it (54–59):

> θεὸς δ' ὑπὸ καλὸν ἄειδεν
> ἐξ αὐτοσχεδίης πειρώμενος, ἠύτε κοῦροι
> ἡβηταὶ θαλίῃσι παραιβόλα κερτομέουσιν,
> ἀμφὶ Δία Κρονίδην καὶ Μαιάδα καλλιπέδιλον,
> ὡς πάρος ὠρίζεσκον ἑταιρείῃ φιλότητι,
> ἥν τ' αὐτοῦ γενεὴν <u>ὀνομακλυτὸν ἐξονομάζων</u>.

(As he tested it [the lyre], the god sang a sweet, impromptu song, the way young men bandy insults at festivals. His song was about Zeus, son of Cronus, and fair-sandalled Maia, and the light talk the lovers spoke before, in the intimacy of their lovemaking, all this as he narrated, name by name, the famous story [*onoma*klyton ex*onomazōn*] of his own begetting.)

---

[12] The tragic dimensions of this realization in the *Iliad* are finely summed up by MacCary (1982: 42): "What we appreciate in the *Iliad* is our own inability to define ourselves in any terms but those provided by our society, *and that therein true alienation lies.*"

The humanly impossible dream continues as he proceeds to establish his own place in the society of the gods, on his own terms, paradoxically by the exercise of the very same antisocial skills given to Autolycus, *kleptosynē* and *horkos*, showing himself to be not only *polytropos* but *autotropos*, capable of the absolutely unique (. . . οἷά τ' ἐπειγόμενος δολιχὴν ὁδόν, αὐτοτροπήσας, 86).[13] The vision of such accomplishments tends to energize human initiative and imaginative tactic-taking, but at the same time defines the thing we call necessity, for the accomplishments are set as far beyond the possibility of human grasp as the gods' life is free of pain and death.

The names of the hero thus represent a polarity analogous to that within which the poem as a whole hovers, between myth and *Märchen*, nomination recapitulating narration: on the one side, *polytropos* Outis, the name which is no name, which suggests, like the faculty of *mētis*, the ability to assume an infinite negativity beyond categorization and boundaries in order to change creatively the face of things; and on the other side Odysseus *odyssamenos, polyarētos, Epēritos*, object of general wrath, himself ranged against others, but fixed by being the clear object of society's unambiguous wrath, bound by having a name that can be cursed. The same two poles between which the character of Odysseus ranges and within which it is defined are further suggested by the formulaic epithets used of him exclusively and with high frequency, on the one hand πολύμητις and πολυμήχανος, easy semantic transformations of *polytropos*, and on the other hand πολύτλας: subject of teeming inventiveness and of active ingenuity, object of a host of troubles to be endured.

We should not conclude our long investigation of the name of Odysseus without having a look at the most recent etymological speculation on the subject, keeping in mind

---

[13] If that is what this *hapax legomenon* really means. See *LfgrE*, s.v. αὐτοτροπήσας.

that the framing perspectives of the text and of "scientific" etymology rarely coincide. That they should coincide, however, is a possibility that we should not be too quick to rule out. We have already observed how Palmer and Nagy make what appears to be a morphologically unimpeachable case for the etymology of Achilles from *Ἀχίλαϝος 'he who brings distress to the people', and how in their view that name semantically condenses and recapitulates the central theme of the *Iliad*. Thus the larger evidential frame of the science of etymology (if indeed it is a science) appears to yield results identical to those an "unscientific" reading might readily produce from what looks like deliberate paronomasia in the first several lines of the proem of the *Iliad* (see above, p. 114). Can anything like that be mined from the name of Odysseus?

So far, nothing corresponding to it has appeared in Linear B tablets in the way that *akireu* yields *Akhilleus*. But Palmer[14] argues that Odysseus's name preserves linguistic elements later discarded from ordinary speech, and that certain morphological and lexical facts bespeak a coinage considerably older than the Linear B tablets. He analyzes the name as a combination of verbal prefix + present stem + the suffix *-eus* to yield *o-dukj-eus* 'he who leads forth'. The verbal prefix *o-*, meaning "on to" or "in to," as in ὀτρύνω 'urge on' and ὀκέλλω 'run (a ship) aground', seems to be archaic and uncommon even in the tablets, and the Indo-European root **deuk-*, which is so common elsewhere (Lat. *dūco*, Eng. *tug*, etc.), was replaced in Greek by ἄγω and ἐλαύνω. The present stem, represented by the transcription *dukj-*, with the zero grade would be a common type represented, for example, by βαίνω (from $*g^w m\text{-}j\text{-}$, with zero grade of the root $*g^w em\text{-}$ 'go, come'). And for the suffix *-eus* added directly to the stem, compare *Epeigeus* 'he who presses hard in pursuit', *epekeu* in the tablets, and the name of a Myrmidon in the *Iliad* (16.571).

[14] Palmer 1980: 36, 98; see also Chantraine 1968–80 s.v.; see Risch 1974: 158, for first speculation on this idea.

All of this becomes even more interesting when we consider the name of Laertes from the same perspective. Palmer derives it from *Lawo-er-tā* 'he who urges on the people', the second element preserving an obsolete verbal root *er-* attested in Hesychius (ἔρετο· ὡρμήθη) and apparently replaced by the extended forms ἐρέθω and ἐρεθίζω. The name as such does not appear in Linear B tablets, but a compound with the same elements reversed has been read out of *etirawo, Ertilāwos*, meaning the same thing. Thus both *Laertes* and *Odysseus* show elements that are already archaic in Homer's Greek. What is more striking, they follow a pattern of naming to which we have already adverted and according to which the son is given a name approximately synonymous with that of his father. Strangely, Palmer does not mention this, even though he notes (1980: 35–36) the same phenomenon in the names of the Atreidae, *Mene-lāwos* 'he who makes the people stand fast' and Aga-men-mōn (with metathesis) or *Aga-memn-ōn* (with reduplication of the root *men-*) 'he who stands fast exceedingly,' sons of *Atreus* from *a-tres-* 'not running away'.

Should we read in the minor theme of Odysseus's unavailing leadership of his men an all but buried trace of a once-significant name O-dukj-eus, a relationship analogous to that discovered by Palmer and Nagy in the name and story of Achilles? Can this be said to surface faintly and momentarily where the proem mentions Odysseus's concern for his companions (1.5–6)?

ἀρνύμενος . . . νόστον ἑταίρων.
ἀλλ' οὐδ' ὣς ἑτάρους ἐρρύσατο, ἱέμενός περ.

However these questions are answered, I find a thematically richer reading by comparing these etymologies, both of which suggest energy, vigor, and initiative, with the dramatic situations in which we find Odysseus and Laertes at the beginning and end of the poem. At the beginning of the poem, "He who leads forth" and "He who urges the people on" are, like poor Argus, in conditions that ironically belie their names. "He who leads forth" is enclosed against his will in the caves of Calypso, and "He who urges the people on" lies immobilized in the country, no longer goes to the town or communes with the *lāos*, is confined in squalid torpor by his own choice. But in the closing sequence of the whole poem, father and son, in arms with their small band for war with the suitors' relatives, reinvest their names with significance, reenacting etymology. And as they sally forth, it is Odukjeus who leads them (24.501):

ὦϊξάν ῥα θύρας, ἐκ δ' ἤϊον, ἦρχε δ' Ὀδυσσεύς.

Making "scientific" etymology one of many possible frames of our reading may permit us to see in ἦρχε the vague trace of an Indo-European hero and his tale. Although that yields relatively thin returns—what Homeric hero is not in some sense a leader?—still it should not be discounted, for it coheres with the energetic forwardness with which the text more explicitly and repeatedly endows Odysseus, from his youthful heroics on Parnassus, first (*prōtistos*) in the assault on the boar, up to the present moment in the action. But far and away more prominent, I would argue, is the Autolycan etymology. For at no point in the career of Odysseus is his name more fully realized than in the closing lines of the poem; nowhere is he more *polyarētos*, more *odyssamenos*, the community marshalled against him, and he against them in *neikos*, mutual conflict. His furious assault is checked only by a lightning-bolt of Zeus and the warning of Athena, couched in words that synonymously reiterate her pun in book 1 (ὠδύσαο, Ζεῦ, 62), that he courts the anger of Zeus (24.542–43):

ἴσχεο, παῦε δὲ νεῖκος ὁμοιΐου πτολέμοιο,
μή πώς τοι Κρονίδης κεχολώσεται εὐρύοπα Ζεύς.

(Hold yourself back! Stop this strife of warfare, or wide-browed *Zeus*, son of Cronus, may *grow angry* with you.)

In other words, if in book 1 Odysseus is not, as his name suggests, the object of Zeus's anger, here at the end he

shows himself to be the kind of man who could be. Closure
here is achieved not by the syntagmatic completion of all
"narrative trajectories,"[15] that is, by the achievement or final frustration of goals generated within the narrative, but
by paradigmatic ring-composition: verbally in the synon-
ymy of κεχολώσεται and ὠδύσαο; dramatically in the constraint (ἴσχεο, παῦε) here imposed upon the same *polytropos* "held back" in Calypso's hollow caves in book 1 (ἔρυκε,
14; compare ἴσχει, 4.558 = 5.15 = 17.144). But the constraint is only temporary. The lightning-bolt of Zeus marks
a narrative colon, not a period. The tale opens with its
hero grounded, enclosed, enveloped; it closes with its hero
launched in full assault "like a high flying eagle" (ὥς τ᾽
αἰετὸς ὑψιπετήεις, 24.538), then temporarily checked,
but facing, in the *ametrētos ponos*, the indefinite labor imposed by the prophecy of Tiresias, an open field of possibilities, a fresh story, his goal, unlike Ithaca, fixed neither
in space nor in time nor by name: to find a land and people unnamed, like himself at the beginning of his story, a
land and people to be recognized only if and when his
shouldered oar is given a strange name never before used
of it or of the winnowing-fan it resembles. At such a point,
if he ever reaches it, Odysseus is to fix his oar in the earth,
permanently to immobilize the instrument of propulsion,
to ground the organ of flight (ἐρετμά, τά τε πτερὰ νηυσὶ
πέλονται, 11.125): perfect metaphor for the cessation of
the narrative trajectory—the poem's ἔπεα πτερόεντα—
and of the life it signifies, match for the stilled oar on the
burial mound of Elpenor, "man of desire," or the fairy
ship of the Phaeacians, fearless and swift as thought,
steered, without helm or helmsman, like the hero it whisks
home, by the knowledge of the minds and cities of men,

[15] On the concept of "narrative trajectory," see Greimas and Courtés
1982: 207–8. "A *narrative trajectory* is a hypotactic series of either simple
or complex narrative programs, that is, a logical chain in which each narrative program is presupposed by another, presupposing, narrative program" (207).

but doomed finally to be rooted forever, frozen in stone (8.557-71).

To what does the name "Odysseus" refer?[16] Early in our investigation of naming we indicated that a name without an identifying description would be inflated currency. It may initiate or sustain a narrative by specifying a yet-in-definite subject of which attributes and actions can be predicated. The unfamiliar suppression of the name in its expected location draws attention to this phenomenon, containing the potentiality for becoming a reflection on the polytropic character of the narrative act itself, in a story already otherwise and more explicitly preoccupied with the telling of tales, true and false. For the audience that carries to the narrative transaction identifying descriptions for the name "Odysseus" from other tales, this grand tale seems to be controlling and perhaps, if need be, correcting them, the way Odysseus himself corrects the view the Phaeacians have of him as largely *ptoliporthios* by asserting the preeminence of his *dolos* and by telling a long tale devoted largely to his *mētis*. In the long run, what identifying description will serve more reliably than the *Odyssey* itself? For the poem sustains without final resolution an alternation between myth and *Märchen*, between the narrative of desire frustrated and the narrative of desire fulfilled, between the story of a versatile agent and the story of an enduring patient. That alternation has its analogue in the tension within the hero's names—*polytropos* 'much-turning' and 'much-turned,' *odyssamenos* 'hating' and 'hated'—and in the tension between his names—*ptoliporthios* versus Outis, *polymēchanos* versus *polytlas*, the last two epithets used of him. Nowhere are the contending Bakhtinian voices more evident than in the closing lines of the

---

[16] We should by now have left behind us a simplistic notion of reference. For a good study of the problems of reference, especially in literary and historical texts, see Ricoeur 1988: 157ff.; Whiteside and Issacharoff 1987 (esp. their bibliography); Castañeda 1979; Pavel 1979; Pagnini 1987: ch. 4; and Searle 1975.

poem, where these two epithets are ranged ironically against one another: Odysseus is called *polytlas* (24.537), the epithet suggesting endurance in the face of the inevitable, at the very moment when, active master of the situation, he launches into action; he is called *polymētis* (24.542), suggesting control of the world by infinite cunning, in the context of its curtailment (ἴσχεο, παῦε, 543) as it confronts its limits.

To what does the name "Odysseus" refer? In a sense, it refers to a broadened sense of the self. In comparison with the *Iliad*, the *Odyssey* seems to present a paradigm of human potential that is considerably less deterministic. Instead of the narrow quest for an abiding *kleos* beyond death, that attempt permanently to fix the name in the community through competitive excellence, the poet's realization of his capacity to predicate nearly anything of his subject creates a "character" of infinite variety, whose self-chosen anonymity, identified with *mētis*, becomes a paradigm, when taken over into "real life," for a subtler ideology of the self still embryonic in the *Iliad*, a sense of self with depth. In the self-consciousness of his art, the storyteller creates a subject at once *polytropos* and *outis*, a secret base for open predication, rather than a determinate sum of predicates, and thus presents a paradigm for a view of the self as capable, dynamic, free, rather than fixed, fated, defined. This is not a creation *ex nihilo* (ἐξ οὔτιδος!) but the hard-won product of a persistent dialectic between two Bakhtinian voices. The pierced border and the exchange of injury that Odysseus's name suggests, the dialectic between the unconventional trickster and both the world of nature and normative society: all this reiterates metaphorically the dialectic between necessity and freedom, between a sense of the self as object and a sense of the self as subject, as patient and as agent, man in the middle voice. The *Odyssey* shows major gains on the side of freedom and human potential resulting from this dialectic. It has its analogue at the level of the narrative act in the dialectic between the poet's sense of power over his material on the one side, and the pressures of tradition and verisimilitude coming from outside the narrative on the other. The *Odyssey* itself shows us two views of poetic activity, distinguished from one another by the extent of their subservience to that outside pressure, and gives heavier weight, I would argue against the Parryites, to the second. One is a discourse of *representation*, embodied in the blind Phaeacian bard Demodocus, who gracefully repeats a fixed tradition given to him in inspiration by the Muses to keep the past intact; the other is a discourse of *production*, embodied in Odysseus himself, who freely designs fictions out of his own ingenuity to control present circumstance and to serve his purpose for the future. It also has its analogue on the divine plane in the dialectic between Poseidon, who stands for all the world's hard inertia, and the daughter of Metis, Athena, mistress of pragmatic intelligence, divine counterpart of her mortal protégé, and embodiment of the narrative impulse itself, for it is she who is the prime mover of the action, the impetus that keeps it going, the frequent internal expedient against the pressures of verisimilitude, and the force that brings it to its counterfeit conclusion.

To what does the name "Odysseus" refer? In the final analysis, it refers in a sense to no one, to nothing, but nothing in the rich sense of the zero-degree, which signifies not simply nonbeing, but potentiality, what it means for the empty subject of narrative to take on any predication or attribute, for Athena to simulate anyone (13.313), for dormant Proteus to become anything that is, for Outis to become *polytropos*. It is the point where Sisyphus, true progenitor of Odysseus, unlike his immoblized companions Tityus and Tantalus, rebounds against failure, forever resilient even in the realm of death to face Krataiis, the ruthless power of necessity. It is the zero-point where every story begins, the zero-point where every story ends, rich with the possibility of another beginning.

BIBLIOGRAPHY

Ameis, K. F., and C. Hentze. 1879–80. *Anhang zu Homers Odyssee.* 4 vols. Leipzig.

———. 1908–20. *Homers Odyssee.* Rev. P. Cauer. 2 vols. Leipzig.

Amory, Anne. 1963. "The Reunion of Odysseus and Penelope." In *Essays on the Odyssey,* edited by C. H. Taylor, 100–121. Bloomington.

Atkinson, Paul. 1985. *Language, Structure and Reproduction.* London.

Auerbach, Erich. 1953. "Odysseus' Scar." In *Mimesis: The Representation of Reality in Western Literature,* trans. Willard Trask. Princeton.

Austin, Norman. 1972. "Name Magic in the *Odyssey.*" *California Studies in Classical Antiquity* 5: 1–19.

———. 1981. "Odysseus Polytropos: Man of Many Minds." *Arche* 6: 40–52.

Bakhtin, Mikhail M. 1981. *The Dialogic Imagination: Four Essays.* Ed. Michael Holquist, trans. Caryl Emerson and Michael Holquist. Austin and London.

Barthes, Roland. 1970. *Elements of Semiology* (printed together with *Writing Degree Zero*). Trans. Annette Lavers and Colin Smith. Boston.

———. 1972. *Mythologies.* Trans. Annette Lavers. New York.

———. 1974. *S/Z.* Trans. Richard Miller. New York.

———. 1983. *The Fashion System.* Trans. Matthew Ward and Richard Howard. New York.

Bascom, William. 1965. "The Forms of Folklore: Prose Narratives." *Journal of American Folklore* 78: 3–20.

Bassett, S. E. 1933. "The Fate of the Phaeacians." *Classical Philology* 28: 305–7.

Benveniste, E. 1966. "Actif et moyen dans le verbe." In *Problèmes de la linguistique générale,* 168–75. Paris.

Bergren, Ann. 1983. "Odyssean Temporality: Many (Re)turns." In *Approaches to Homer,* edited by Carl Rubino and Cynthia Shelmerdine, 38–73. Austin and London.

Bettelheim, Bruno. 1976. *The Uses of Enchantment: The Meaning and Importance of Fairy Tales.* New York.

Bolling, G. M. 1925. *External Evidence for Interpolation in Homer.* Oxford.

Bottigheimer, Ruth B. 1987. *Grimms' Bad Girls and Bold Boys: The Moral and Social Vision of the Tales.* New Haven.

Bourdieu, Pierre. 1977. *Outline of a Theory of Practice.* Trans. Richard Nice. Cambridge.

Bourdieu, Pierre, and Jean-Claude Passeron. 1977. *Reproduction in Education, Society and Culture.* London and Beverly Hills.

Bremond, Claude. 1973. *Logique du récit.* Paris.

Bruner, Jerome. 1986. *Actual Minds, Possible Worlds.* Cambridge, Mass. and London.

Bühler, Charlotte. 1958. *Das Märchen und die Phantasie des Kindes.* Munich.

Burrell, David, and Stanley Hauerwas. 1976. "From System to Story: An Alternative Pattern for Rationality in Ethics." In *The Roots of Ethics,* edited by Daniel Callahan and H. Tristram Engelhardt, 75–116. New York and London.

Calhoun, G. M. 1939. "Homer's Gods—Myth and Märchen." *American Journal of Philology* 60: 1–28.

Cassirer, Ernst. 1955. *The Philosophy of Symbolic Forms II: Mythical Thought.* Trans. Ralph Manheim. New Haven.

Castañeda, Hector-Neri. 1979. "Fiction and Reality: Their Fundamental Connections." *Poetics* 8: 31–62.

———. 1985. "The Semantics and the Causal Roles of Proper Names in Our Thinking of Particulars." *Philosophy and Phenomenological Research* 46: 91–113.

Chantraine, Pierre. 1958. *Grammaire homérique I: phonétique et morphologie.* 3rd ed. Paris.

———. 1963. *Grammaire homérique II: syntaxe.* 2nd ed. Paris.

———. 1968–80. *Dictionnaire étymologique de la langue grecque: histoire des mots.* Paris.

Chatman, Seymour. 1978. *Story and Discourse: Narrative Structure in Fiction and Film.* Ithaca, N.Y.

Chisholm, Roderick M. 1981. *The First Person: An Essay on Reference and Intentionality.* Minneapolis.

Cixous, Hélène. 1974. "The Character of 'Character.'" *New Literary History* 5: 383–402.

Clay, Jenny Strauss. 1983. *The Wrath of Athena: Gods and Men in the Odyssey.* Princeton.

Cocchiara, Giuseppe. 1981. *The History of Folklore in Europe.* Trans. John N. McDaniel. Philadelphia.

Cooper, David E. 1986. *Metaphor*. (Aristotelian Society Series, vol. 5. Oxford.

Culler, Jonathan. 1975. *Structuralist Poetics*. London.

————. 1981. *The Pursuit of Signs: Semiotics, Literature, Deconstruction*. Ithaca, N.Y.

————. 1982. *On Deconstruction: Theory and Criticism after Structuralism*. Ithaca, N.Y.

Davis, Lennard J. 1987. *Resisting Novels: Ideology and Fiction*. New York and London.

De Certeau, Michel. 1984. *The Practice of Everyday Life*. Trans. Steven F. Rendall. Berkeley.

De Jong, Irene J. F. 1985. "Eurycleia and Odysseus' Scar." *Classical Quarterly*, n.s. 35: 517–18.

De Man, Paul. 1982. "The Resistance to Theory." *Yale French Studies* 63: 3–20.

De Vries, Jan. 1954. *Betrachtungen zum Märchen, besonders in seinem Verhältnis zu Heldensage und Mythos*. Folklore Fellows Communications 150. Helsinki.

————. 1958. "The Problem of the Fairy Tale." *Diogenes* 22: 1–15.

————. 1961. "Märchen, Mythos und Mythenmärchen." *Internationaler Kongress der Volkerzählungsforscher, Kiel 1959, Vorträge und Referate*. Berlin.

Denniston, J. D. 1934. *Greek Particles*. Oxford.

Derrida, Jacques. 1970. "Structure, Sign, and Play in the Discourse of the Human Sciences." In Macksey and Donato 1970, pp. 247–65.

————. 1976. *Of Grammatology*. Trans. Gayatri Chakravorty Spivak. Baltimore.

Destouches, Jean Louis. 1950. *Cours de logique et philosophie générale*. Paris.

Detienne, Marcel, and Jean-Pierre Vernant. 1978. *Cunning Intelligence in Greek Culture and Society*. Trans. Janet Lloyd. Atlantic Highlands, N.J.

Devereux, Georges. 1957. "Penelope's Character." *Psychoanalytic Quarterly* 26: 378–86.

————. 1968. "Considérations psychanalytiques sur la divination particulièrment chez les Grecs." In *La Divination II*, edited by André Caquot and Marcel Leibovici, 449–71. Paris.

Diano, Carlo. 1968. "La poetica dei Feaci." In *Saggezza e poetiche degli antichi*. Venice.

Dimock, George E. 1956. "The Name of Odysseus," *Hudson Review* 9: 52–70.

———. 1989. *The Unity of the Odyssey.* Amherst, Mass.

Docherty, Thomas. 1983. *Reading (Absent) Character: Towards a Theory of Characterization in Fiction.* Oxford.

Dodds, E. R. 1957. *The Greeks and the Irrational.* Berkeley.

Dornseiff, Franz. 1937. "Odysseus' letzte Fahrt." *Hermes* 72: 351–55.

Duckworth, G. E. 1933. *Foreshadowing and Suspense in the Epics of Homer, Apollonius, and Vergil.* Princeton.

Ducrot, Oswald, and Tzvetan Todorov. 1979. *Encyclopedic Dictionary of the Sciences of Language.* Trans. Catherine Porter. Baltimore.

Dundes, Alan. 1968. Introduction to Propp 1968, pp. xi–xvii.

Durante, Marcello. 1971–76. *Sulla preistoria della tradizione poetica greca.* 2 vols. Rome.

Eagleton, Terry. 1983. *Literary Theory: An Introduction.* Minneapolis.

Eco, Umberto. 1976. *A Theory of Semiotics.* Bloomington.

Edwards, Anthony T. 1985. *Achilles in the Odyssey.* Beiträge zur klassischen Philologie, 171. Königstein/Ts.

Edwards, Mark. 1987. *Homer: Poet of the Iliad.* Baltimore and London.

Ehnmark, E. 1935. *The Idea of God in Homer.* Uppsala.

Evans, Gareth. 1977. "The Causal Theory of Names." In *Naming, Necessity, and Natural Kinds,* edited by Stephen P. Schwartz, 192–215. Ithaca, N.Y.

———. 1982. *The Varieties of Reference.* Oxford.

Felson-Rubin, Nancy. 1987. "Penelope's Perspective: Character from Plot." In *Homer: Beyond Oral Poetry. Recent Trends in Homeric Interpretation,* edited by J. M. Bremer, I.J.F. de Jong, and J. Kalff, pp. 61–83. Amsterdam.

Fernández-Galiano, Manuel, and Alfred Heubeck. 1986. *Omero, Odissea: libri XXI—XXIV.* Trans. G. Aurelio Privitera. Milan.

Finley, M. I. 1978. *The World of Odysseus.* 2nd ed. Middlesex and New York.

Finnegan, Ruth. 1970. *Oral Literature in Africa.* Oxford.

———. 1977. *Oral Poetry: Its Nature, Signficance and Social Context.* Cambridge.

Finsler, G. 1918. *Homer.* 2 vols. Leipzig.

Fitch, G. W. 1987. *Naming and Believing.* Dordrecht and Boston.

Flacelière, R. 1971. *L'Amour en Grèce*. Paris.

Focke, F. 1943. *Die Odyssee*. Stuttgart and Berlin.

Foucault, Michel. 1970. *The Order of Things*. Trans. Alan Sheridan, with foreword by Foucault. London and New York.

Frazer, P. M., and E. Matthews, eds. 1987. *A Lexicon of Greek Personal Names*. Vol. 1: *The Aegean Islands, Cyprus, Cyrenaica*. Oxford.

Gass, William H. 1970. *Fiction and the Figures of Life*. New York.

Genette, Gerard. 1968. "Vraisemblance et motivation." *Communications* 11: 5–21.

Goldhill, Simon. 1984. "Exegesis: Oedipus (R)ex." *Arethusa* 17: 177–200.

Greimas, A. J., and J. Courtés. 1982. *Semiotics and Language: An Analytical Dictionary*. Trans. Larry Crist, Daniel Patte, and others. Bloomington.

Greimas, A. J. 1983. *Structural Semantics: an Attempt at a Method*. Lincoln, Neb. and London.

Gurvitch, Georges. 1971. *The Social Frameworks of Knowledge*. Trans. Margaret and Kenneth Thompson. Oxford.

Hainsworth, John B. 1986. *Omero, Odissea: libri V–VIII*. Trans. G. Aurelio Privitera. 2nd ed. Milan.

Hansen, W. F. 1977. "Odysseus' Last Journey." *Quaderni Urbinati di Studi Classici* 24: 27–48.

Harsh, Philip H. 1950. "Penelope and Odysseus in *Od.* 19." *American Journal of Philology* 71: 1–21.

Heitsch, Ernst. 1964. "Tlemosyne," *Hermes* 92: 257–64.

Heubeck, Alfred. 1986. *Omero, Odissea: libri IX–XII*. Trans. G. Aurelio Privitera. 2nd ed. Milan.

Heubeck, Alfred, and Stephanie West. 1986. *Omero, Odissea: libri I–IV*. Trans. G. Aurelio Privitera. 2nd ed. Milan.

Hoekstra, A. 1987. *Omero, Odissea: libri XIII–XVI*. Trans. G. Aurelio Privitera. 2nd ed. Milan.

Hoelscher, Uvo. 1978. "The Transformation from Folk-Tale to Epic." In *Homer: Tradition and Invention*, edited by Bernard Fenik, 51–67. Leiden.

Honti, Hans. 1931. *Volksmärchen und Heldensage*. Folklore Fellows Communication, 95. Helsinki.

Horn, Laurence R. 1989. *A Natural History of Negation*. Chicago.

Housman, A. E. 1972. *The Classical Papers of A. E. Housman*. 3 vols. Edited by J. Diggle and F.R.D. Goodyear. Cambridge.

176 BIBLIOGRAPHY

Howell, Robert. 1979. "Fictional Objects: How They Are and How They Are Not." *Poetics* 8: 129–77.

Jakobson, Roman. 1978. *Six Lectures on Sound and Meaning.* Trans. John Mepham. Preface by Claude Lévi-Strauss. Sussex.

———. 1985. "Subliminal Verbal Patterning in Poetry." In *Verbal Art, Verbal Sign, Verbal Time*, edited by in Krystyna Pomorska and Stephen Rudy, 59–68. Minneapolis.

Jakobson, Roman. 1987. *Language in Literature.* Edited by Krystyna Pomorska and Stephen Rudy. Cambridge, Mass. and London.

Jameson, Frederic. 1972. *The Prison House of Language.* Princeton.

Jolles, André. 1956. *Einfache Formen.* 2nd ed. Halle.

Kakridis, H. J. 1963. *La Notion de l'amitié et de l'hospitalité chez Homère.* Thessaloniki.

Kermode, Frank. 1966. *The Sense of an Ending: Studies in the Theory of Fiction.* Oxford.

———. 1983. *The Art of Telling: Essays on Fiction.* Cambridge, Mass.

Kirchhoff, A. 1879. *Die homerische Odyssee.* Berlin.

Kirk, G. S. 1962. *The Songs of Homer.* Cambridge.

———. 1970. *Myth: Its Meaning and Functions in Ancient and Other Cultures.* Berkeley and Cambridge.

Kripke, Saul. 1972. "Naming and Necessity." In *Semantics of Natural Languages*, edited by D. Davidson and G. Harman, 763–69. Dordrecht.

Kühner., R., P. Blass, and B. Gerth. 1890–1904. *Ausführliche Grammatik der griechischen Sprache.* Hanover.

Kurrik, Maire Jaanus. 1979. *Literature and Negation.* New York.

Lehmann, Winfred P. 1974. *Proto-Indo-European Syntax.* Austin and London.

Lévi-Strauss, Claude. 1950. "Introduction à l'oeuvre de Marcel Mauss." In Marcel Mauss, *Sociologie et anthropologie.* Paris.

———. 1963. *Structural Anthropology.* Trans. C. Jacobson and B. Grundfest Schoepf. New York.

———. 1966. *The Savage Mind.* Chicago.

———. 1969. *The Raw and the Cooked.* Trans. John and Doreen Weightman. New York.

———. 1973. *From Honey to Ashes.* Trans. John and Doreen Weightman. New York.

———. 1978. *The Origin of Table Manners.* Trans. John and Doreen Weightman. New York.

———. 1981. *The Naked Man*. Trans. John and Doreen Weightman. New York.

Levy, Harry L. 1963. "The Odyssean Suitors and Host-Guest Relationship." *Transactions and Proceedings of the American Philological Association* 95: 145–53.

Lewis, Phillip. 1982. "The Post-Structuralist Condition." *Diacritics* (Spring): 2–24.

Lexikon des frügriechischen Epos 1955–. = *(LfgrE)*. Edited by Snell and H. Erbse. Göttingen.

Linsky, Leonard. 1977. *Names and Descriptions*. Chicago.

Lord, Albert B. 1960. *The Singer of Tales*. Cambridge, Mass.

Lowenthal, David. 1985. *The Past Is a Foreign Country*. Cambridge.

Lüthi, Max. 1964. *Das Europäische Volksmärchen: Form und Wesen*. 4th ed. Bern and Munich.

———. 1970. *Volkliteratur und Hochliteratur: Menschenbild, Thematik, Formtreben*. Bern and Munich.

Lynn-George, Michael. 1988. *Epos: Word, Narrative and the Iliad*. Atlantic Highlands, N.J.

Lyons, John. 1968. *Introduction to Theoretical Linguistics*. Cambridge.

———. 1977. *Semantics*. 2 vols. Cambridge.

MacCary, W. T. 1982. *Childlike Achilles: Ontogeny and Philogeny in the Iliad*. New York.

Macksey, Richard, and Eugenio Donato. 1970. *The Languages of Criticism and the Sciences of Man: the Structuralist Controversy*. Baltimore.

Marot, K. 1960. "Odysseus-Ulixes." *Acta Antiqua* 8: 1–6.

Merry, W. W. 1878, 1887. *Odyssey*. 2 vols. Oxford.

Mühlestein, Hugo. 1987. *Homerische Namenstudien*. Frankfurt am Main.

Murray, Penelope. 1981. "Poetic Inspiration in Early Greece." *Journal of Hellenic Studies* 101: 87–100.

Nagy, Gregory. 1976. "The Name of Achilles: Etymology and Epic." In *Studies in Greek, Italic, and Indo-European Linguistics: Offered to Leonard R. Palmer*, edited by Anna Morpurgo Davies and Wolfgang Meid, 209–37. Innsbruck.

———. 1979. *The Best of the Achaeans: Concepts of the Hero in Archaic Greek Poetry*. Baltimore.

———. 1983. "*Sēma* and *Noēsis*: Some Illustrations." *Arethusa* 16: 35–56.

Needham, Rodney. 1983. *Against the Tranquillity of Axions*. Berkeley.

Page, Denys. 1955. *The Homeric Odyssey*. Oxford.

———. 1972. *Folktales in the Odyssey*. Cambridge, Mass.

Pagnini, Marcello. 1987. *The Pragmatics of Literature*. Trans. Nancy Jones-Henry. Bloomington and Indianapolis.

Palmer, L. R. 1963a. *The Interpretation of Mycenaean Greek Texts*. Oxford.

———. 1963b. "The Language of Homer." In *A Companion to Homer*, edited by A.J.B. Wace and Frank H. Stubbings 75–178. New York and London.

———. 1980. *The Greek Language*. Atlantic Highlands, N.J.

Palmer, Richard E. 1969. *Hermeneutics: Interpretation Theory in Schleiermacher, Dilthey, Heidegger, and Gadamer*. Evanston, Ill.

Pavel, Thomas G. 1979. "Fiction and the Causal Theory of Names." *Poetics* 8: 179–91.

———. 1985. "Literary Narratives." In *Discourse and Literature*, edited by Teun A. van Dijk, 85–104. Amsterdam and Philadelphia.

Peradotto, John. 1974. "*Odyssey* 8: 564–71: Verisimilitude, Narrative Analysis, and Bricolage," *Texas Studies in Literature and Language* 15: 803–32.

———. 1977. "Oedipus and Erichthonius: Some Observations on Paradigmatic and Syntagmatic Order." *Arethusa* 10: 85–101.

———. 1979. "Originality and Intentionality." In *Arktouros: Hellenic Studies Presented to Bernard M. W. Knox*, edited by G. Bowersock, W. Burkert, and M. Putnam, 3–11. Berlin and New York.

———. 1983. "Texts and Unrefracted Facts: Philology, Hermeneutics and Semiotics." *Arethusa* 16: 15–33.

———. 1986. "Prophecy Degree Zero: Tiresias and the End of the *Odyssey*." In *Oralità: Cultura, Letteratura, Discorso*, edited by Bruno Gentili and Giuseppe Paioni, 429–59. Atti del Convegno Internazionale, Urbino 1980. Rome.

Pfeiffer, Rudolf. 1968–76. *History of Classical Scholarship*. 2 vols. Oxford.

Powell, Barry. 1970. "Narrative Pattern in the Homeric Narrative of Menelaus." *Transactions and Proceedings of the American Philological Association* 101: 419–31.

Prado, C. G. 1984. *Making Believe: Philosophical Reflections on Fiction*. Westport, Conn.

Propp, Vladímir. 1968. *Morphology of the Folktale.* 2nd ed. Trans. Laurence Scott. Bibliographical and Special Series of the American Folklore Society, 10. Austin and London.

Pucci, Pietro. 1982. "The Proem of the *Odyssey*." *Arethusa* 15: 39–62.

————. 1986. "Les Figures de la Métis dans l'*Odyssée*." *Metis* 1: 7–28.

————. 1987. *Odysseus Polutropos: Intertextual Readings in the Odyssey and the Iliad.* Ithaca, N.Y.

Radermacher, Ludwig. 1916. *Die Erzählungen der Odyssee.* Sitzungsberichte der Kais. Akad. der Wissenschaften in Wien, Phil.-Hist. Klass, 178. Vienna.

Rank, L. P. 1951. *Etymologiseering en verwante Verschijnselen bij Homeros.* Utrecht.

Rank, Otto. 1919. *Psychoanalytische Beiträge zur Mythenforschung.* Leipzig and Vienna.

Redfield, James M. 1975. *Nature and Culture in the Iliad: The Tragedy of Hector.* Chicago.

Ricoeur, Paul. 1976. *Interpretation Theory: Discourse and the Surplus of Meaning.* Fort Worth, Tex.

————. 1984. *Time and Narrative.* Vol. 1. Trans. Kathleen McLaughlin and David Pellauer. Chicago.

————. 1985. *Time and Narrative.* Vol. 2. Trans. Kathleen McLaughlin and David Pellauer. Chicago.

————. 1988. *Time and Narrative.* Vol. 3. Trans. Kathleen Blamey and David Pellauer. Chicago.

Risch, E. 1974. *Wortbildung der homerischen Sprache.* 2nd ed. Berlin.

Róheim, Géza. 1941. "Myth and Folktale." *American Imago* 2: 266–79.

Röhrich, Lutz. 1956. *Märchen und Wirklichkeit.* Wiesbaden.

Rose, Gilbert P. 1969. "The Unfriendly Phaeacians." *Transactions and Proceedings of the American Philological Association* 100: 387–406.

Rose, Peter W. 1988. "Thersites and the Plural Voices of Homer." *Arethusa* 21: 5–25.

Rouget, Gilbert. 1985. *Music and Trance: A Theory of the Relations between Music and Possession.* Trans. Brunhilde Biebuyck. Chicago.

Russo, Joseph. 1968. "Homer against His Tradition." *Arion* 7: 275–95.

Russo, Joseph. 1982. "Interview and Aftermath: Dream, Fantasy, and Intuition in *Odyssey* 19 and 20." *American Journal of Philology* 103: 4–18.

―――. 1985. *Omero, Odissea: libri XVII–XX.* Trans. G. Aurelio Privitera. Milan.

Salvadore, Marcello. 1987. *Il nome, la persona: saggio sull' etimologia antica.* Università di Genova: Pubblicazioni del Dipartimento di Archeologia, Filologia Classica e loro Tradzioni, n.s. 110. Genoa.

Samonà, G. A. 1982. *Gli itinerari sacri dell'aedo: Ricerca storico-religiosa sui cantori omerici.* Rome.

Schein, Seth. 1970. "Odysseus and Polyphemus in the *Odyssey.*" *Greek, Roman and Byzantine Studies* 11: 73–83.

Schlovski, Viktor. 1929. *O teorii prozy.* Moscow. (Translated into German by Gisela Drohla. Frankfurt, 1966.)

Schwartz, E. 1924. *Die Odyssee.* Munich.

Schwyzer, Eduard. 1938. *Griechische Grammatik.* 3 vols. Munich.

Searle, J. R. 1967. "Proper Names and Descriptions." In *The Encyclopedia of Philosophy*, edited by Paul Edwards, 6: 487–91. New York and London.

―――. 1975. "The Logical Status of Fictional Discourse." *New Literary History* 6: 319–32.

―――. 1983. *Intentionality: An Essay in the Philosophy of Mind.* Cambridge.

Sebeok, Thomas A. 1986. *I Think I Am a Verb.* New York and London.

Segal, Charles P. 1962. "The Phaeacians and the Symbolism of Odysseus' Return." *Arion* vol. 1, no. 4: 17–64.

―――. 1983. "*Kleos* and Its Ironies in the *Odyssey.*" *L'Antiquité Classique* 52: 22–47.

Sheridan, Alan. 1980. *Michel Foucault: The Will to Truth.* London and New York.

Shipp, G. P. 1972. *Studies in the Language of Homer.* 2nd ed. Cambridge.

Silk, M. S., and J. P. Stern. 1981. *Nietzsche on Tragedy.* Cambridge.

Smith, Barbara H. 1968. *Poetic Closure: A Study of How Poems End.* Chicago.

Stanford, W. B. 1950. "Homeric Use of πολυ- Compounds." *Classical Philology* 45: 108–10.

―――. 1952. "The Homeric Etymology of the Name Odysseus." *Classical Philology* 47: 209–13.

————., ed. 1965. *The Odyssey of Homer*. 2 vols. Corrected 2nd ed. London and New York.

Sulzberger, M. 1926. "ONOMA EPONYMON: les noms propres chez Homère et dans la mythologie grecque." *Revue des Études Grecques* 39: 385–447.

Svenbro, Jesper. 1976. *La Parole et le marbre: aux origines de la poétique grecque*. Lund.

Tartar, Maria. 1987. *The Hard Facts of the Grimms' Fairy Tales*. Princeton.

Theiler, W. 1950. "Vermutungen zur Odyssee." *Museum Helveticum* 7: 102–22.

————. 1962. "Ilias und Odyssee in der Verflechtung ihres Entstehens." *Museum Helveticum* 19: 1–27.

Thompson, Stith. 1946. *The Folktale*. New York.

Todorov, Tzvetan. 1967. *Littérature et signification*. Paris.

————. 1969. *Grammaire du Décaméron*. The Hague and Paris.

————. 1977. *The Poetics of Prose*. Trans. Richard Howard. Ithaca, N.Y.

————. 1984. *Mikhail Bakhtin: The Dialogical Principle*. Trans. Wlad Godzich. Minneapolis.

Turner, Terence. 1977. "Narrative Structure and Mythopoesis: A Critique and Reformulation of Structuralist Concepts of Myth, Narrative and Poetics." *Arethusa* 10: 103–63.

Tyler, Stephen. 1987. *The Unspeakable: Discourse, Dialogue, and Rhetoric in the Postmodern World*. Madison, Wisc.

Valery, Paul. 1957. *Oeuvres*. 2 vols. Edited by Jean Hytier. Paris.

Van Leeuwen, J. 1917. *Homeri Carmina II: Odyssea*. Leyden.

Vernant, Jean-Pierre. 1975. "Catégories de l'agent et de l'action en Grèce ancienne." In *Langue, discourse, société: pour E. Benveniste*, edited by Julia Kristeva, J.-C. Milner, and Nicolas Ruwet, 365–73. Paris.

Von Beit, Hedwig. 1952–57. *Symbolik des Märchens: Versuch einer Deutung*. 3 vols. Bern.

————. 1965. *Das Märchen*. Bern.

Von der Leyen, Friedrich (with Kurt Schier). 1958. *Das Märchen: Ein Versuch*. 4th ed. Heidelberg.

————. 1959. "Mythus und Märchen." *Deutsche Vierteljahrsschrift für Literaturwissenschaft und Geistesgeschichte* 33: 343–60.

Von der Mühll, P. 1940. "Odyssee." *RE* Supplementband 7. Coll. 696–768. Stuttgart.

————, ed. 1962. *Homeri Odyssea*. Basil.

Waanders, F.M.J. 1983. *The History of Τέλος and Τελέω in Ancient Greek.* Amsterdam.

Wackernagel, J. 1916. *Sprachliche Untersuchungen zu Homer.* Philologische Seminar, Universität Basel, 1. Göttingen.

Whiteside, Anna, and Michael Issacharoff, eds. 1987. *On Referring in Literature.* Bloomington and Indianapolis.

Wilamowitz-Moellendorf, Ulrich von. 1884. *Homerische Untersuchungen.* Berlin.

———. 1927. *Die Heimkehr des Odysseus.* Berlin.

Woodhouse, W. J. 1930. *The Composition of Homer's Odyssey.* Oxford.

Zipes, Jack. 1979. *Breaking the Magic Spell: Radical Theories of Folk and Fairy Tales.* London.

———. 1983. *Fairy Tales and the Art of Subversion.* New York.

Zumthor, Paul. 1983. *Introduction à la poésie orale.* Paris.

INDEX OF HOMERIC PASSAGES CITED OR DISCUSSED

INDEX OF GREEK WORDS

INDEX OF NAMES AND SUBJECTS